# CHOIR IDEAS

(For Choir Members, Directors, Preachers
and Congregations)

# CHOIR IDEAS

## (FOR CHOIR MEMBERS, DIRECTORS, PREACHERS AND CONGREGATIONS)

*By*

FLORA E. BRECK

(Author of *Worship Services and Programs for Beginners*
*Church School Chats for Primary Teaching*
*Special Day Programs and Selections*)

# W. A. WILDE COMPANY

PUBLISHERS                    BOSTON

*Made in the United States of America*

1108655

*Dedicated*
*to*
*All Who Enjoy Hymn-Singing*

# ACKNOWLEDGMENT

Certain publishers have kindly granted me permission to reproduce in this book copyrighted material, and grateful acknowledgment is hereby made to the following for such permissions:

To LORENZ PUBLISHING COMPANY for permission to include a reprint of the following *articles* and hymn of mine appearing in the publications noted:

*A Five-Choir Church,* published November, 1943, in THE CHOIR LEADER;

*After-Service Hymn-Sings,* published March, 1943, in THE CHOIR LEADER;

*Each Esteeming the Other Better Than Himself,* published April, 1950, in THE CHOIR LEADER;

*Featuring Hymn-Anthems,* published August, 1944, in THE CHOIR LEADER;

*Hymn-Sings Help Pay Off Mortgage,* published September, 1944, in THE CHOIR LEADER;

*Illustrated Song Service Attracts,* published November, 1936, in THE CHOIR LEADER;

*Making Church Music a Real Ministry,* pub-

lished November, 1942, in THE CHOIR HER-
ALD;

*Secular Choir Concert Solves Money Problem,*
published September, 1936, in THE CHOIR
LEADER;

*The Power of Sacred Song,* published October,
1950, in THE CHOIR LEADER;

*The Story Back of Gospel Songs,* published
October, 1934, in THE CHOIR LEADER;

*The World's Home Song,* published May, 1947,
in THE CHOIR HERALD.

And the *hymn* I wrote the words of: *Jesus Is
Alive (Easter Salutation),* first appearing in
their "THE VOLUNTEER CHOIR" (March,
1949), and more recently in "LORENZ'S SONG
SPECIALS NO. 2—for Choir Use."

To THE RODEHEAVER HALL-MACK COMPANY
for permission to quote freely from lectures
delivered by the late Charles H. Gabriel on the
theme of Choirs, Choir Leaders, Church Music,
etc. (*Note:* The pamphlet is now out of print, so
I refrain from mentioning the title.)

To my sister, GRACE M. BRECK, for her edito-
rial assistance in connection with certain portions
of this work, my sincere appreciation is acknowledged.

# PREFACE

Members and leaders of volunteer church choirs have opportunity only occasionally to visit other choirs, and to observe at first hand the methods which other choirs have found successful. The purpose of this book is to tell informally something of the experiences of a number of choirs, and to offer suggestions for the successful conduct of choir work. I hope also that the book may bring to pastors and lay workers an increased appreciation of the ministry of music in the church and in the community.

I have intentionally omitted reference to the work done by professional singers in large, wealthy church choirs, as such choirs are not typical. The material presented includes accounts of the work done by average choirs in average churches. The text is not a course in choir directing and singing, but is a little book written in the spirit of, "Let's visit together about choirs."

Through the years I have talked with choir leaders, and have jotted down some of their thoughts and practices on choir and congregational singing which I felt others might find useful; and if any who are engaged in the ministry of music find my book helpful, I shall be glad. There are few kinds of church work which are more important and more spiritually rewarding than the producing of a worthy type of church music.

Flora E. Breck

# CONTENTS

11

# CONTENTS

## Chapter I

# CHURCH MUSIC SHOULD BRING US NEARER TO GOD

"Why is it that the man who sings in the bathtub Sunday morning, so the whole house can hear, is struck dumb when the first hymn is announced in church?" asked Dr. Calvin W. Laufer, Philadelphia "hymn doctor," as he has been called, while leading a conference of preachers and religious song-leaders in Portland, Oregon, sometime ago. "Self-consciousness is the answer," Dr. Laufer declared. "People are afraid of their own voices."

And he explained that this self-consciousness can largely be broken up if the congregation be given the background of the hymns they are about to sing, or if perhaps they are told the story surrounding the writing or composition of the hymn about to be sung. These explanations have real value, he emphasized.

Current trends in hymn-singing and effective methods for securing desired results were dis-

13

cussed by this church educator, and the gist of some of his remarks are included here.

The limited number of hymns which the average congregation sings is to be deplored. A Methodist preacher admitted recently that he used but fifty hymns during an entire church year. Many do not use over sixty. This isn't fair to the hymnology of the church. We could use at least 364 to good advantage. The low number actually used is perhaps due to the lack of appreciation of hymns and hymn-tunes on the part of the average congregation.

Five sharps or flats are not difficult, and yet many musicians steer clear of them. Large and rich sections, also, of the average hymnal are sometimes left untouched. If the congregation but knew more as to how the hymns came into being, a marked difference would be noted in their response. This is why the preacher should sometimes say a word about the birth of the song—it would awaken interest in the number announced.

Some of the old patterns in hymns, too, are monotonous instead of being spontaneous, instead of being born in the heart. At this point Dr. Laufer tapped his pencil on the pulpit table, and asked his hearers to guess what he was "playing." Some answered, "Sun of My Soul"; others said other hymn-tunes, so frequently was this pattern found in the old style of hymn. He declared there should be more change in meter in order to register joyousness, serenity, virility, majesty. Songs of victory, comfort, and cheer supersede the doleful type of old-time church hymns. However, a good many of the very old hymns are beautiful and are still sung with joy today.

As to the kind of Sunday service being prepared, preacher and song-leader should ask themselves, "Am I doing what I should to attain the object of the church service? Do I know just why I use a response here and a prelude there?" Preachers and song-leaders should study just what happens when people worship, then meet these experiences with the kind of service that will support it.

The dignified orderliness of the church service was stressed. Some people object to responses, as being "too ritualistic." However, "a certain service in a certain manner" *is* a "ritual" anyway, so none need fear it. And the present desire is to have a finer ritual than now exists.

Let us analyze the situation. We go to church to worship. And what happens when we worship? Here is a large triangle on the blackboard. Our approach to God (pointing from the base of the triangle to the incline line) is away from the horizontal life. We touch God by coming to church. There are many drawbacks, in present-day activities, to this which prevent people from getting into the spirit of a nearness-to-God feeling. The Sunday newspaper for one. At church we create an atmosphere that will fix the attention on God. The soul is moving up, and God is coming down to meet the soul. Finally they come together: one heart, one mind. And we control the situation by worshipping. A soul-moving prelude helps. There should be a hush and reverence over the entire church at least five minutes while the congregation is assembling. Visiting should not be tolerated at that time. There is a real purpose behind the "sacrament of silence," too, at the close of the church service, and the people should wait for the postlude. Finally each person has, so to speak, come down from the mountain-top experience (as represented by the high point of the church service,—the highest point of the triangle) and gradually comes down to the line of life. The organ music at the close, after the benediction, is supposed to enable the worshippers to face the world with new courage.

But to go back to the subject of the thing which occurs in the church service—the soul seeking

God, and God seeking the soul: opportunity of at least twenty minutes' duration should be given for this in each church service. Hymns should be selected with this in mind. Even in Japan, for instance, their hymnals recognize this movement, and they are including more of worship numbers and hymns of thanksgiving. Usually the hymn-portion of the service suffers for the sermon. The choir should be given more chance, and also the congregation, for adoration through the medium of church music. The preaching should not over-shadow the time for that.

Another tendency in church worship today is enrichment of the inner life through the abiding presence of Jesus. Being renewed daily by the presence and power of the Holy One. Not a far-away Christ, but a by-the-side Companion, as well as Redeemer. The One Who works within us. Therefore the hymns chosen should be those richer in adoration and praise.

And in the new hymnal we note another tend-ency: the section dealing with new world-atti-tudes,—comradeship, friendship, world-brother-hood.

As to the manner of singing: Some ask if the choir should set the tempo of the numbers chosen. The tempo in reality should be determined by the character of the hymn. Joyous hymns are above a modest tempo, for instance. In this connection, it is not always satisfactory to play tunes just as written. You should study what the composer *tried* to say, and assuredly the mere notes do not show *all* the composer felt. Perhaps no two verses are sung in just the same way. The music amplifies the sentiment of the hymn text. Try to express the great idea. Make the music say the thing that the author wrote and that the composer felt. There is quite a tendency in church singing to sing too fast or too slowly. Hymns should be practiced and expressed with the emotion and high purpose as of the composers.

One fault with church music today: too many song-leaders decide in a hurry the hymns to be sung. Instead, the selection should be made by Monday or Tuesday at the latest, the preacher and song-leader cooperating early. The song-leader should be apprized of the major purpose of the forthcoming Sunday's service.

In the choir practice, that group should study the hymns to be used, to see their beauty and feel their wonder. The singers should search their qualities, and the organist should play the music so as to express the relation of the hymn to the music. The person at the organ preaches the Gos-

pel as truly as does the preacher. The organist
will let self go if his heart is in the music. Some
organists *pray before they play* at the organ.
When this is done the congregation waits, hushed,
ready to take up the strains. These "ministers of
music" are *spiritually alive* and impart a real
message.

## Chapter II

## MAKING CHURCH MUSIC
## A REAL MINISTRY

*By* Flora E. Breck

(*This article originally appeared in the magazine,* The Choir Herald, *published by Lorenz.*)

By careful thought, the music of the church may be made as much a blessing as is the spoken word. Sometimes by combining selections, new and impressive song messages are achieved. Beautiful hymns feed the soul, and when a familiar number is used in a fresh, interesting way, new chords are touched. Sometimes even a slight change in the illumination of a church adds richness to the songs being sung.

Those who attend the First Baptist Church of Portland, Ore., find the closing number sung by the choir one of the high points of the church service in the evening. Many enjoy it so much that they ask the choir director, W. H. Hollensted, "What is the name of the hymn benediction you sing?" And Professor Hollensted explains that it is called "The Northfield Benediction." It is the one which starts with the line, "The Lord bless thee and keep thee." Then, when it comes to the line, "The Lord lift up his countenance upon thee," the lights in the church take on a beautiful, subdued, holy quality, suggesting the presence of the Lord. Under the change of light and beautiful music one feels especially His nearness. The impressive effect is indescribable. Some admit they are close to tears. A spoken benediction could be no more helpful than this.

When asked further concerning this number, Professor Hollensted declared, "We used that benediction every Sunday for eight years where I served previously, and we've used it nearly four years in this church." He considers it one of the *durable* hymns, of which no one tires, as the hearers love it increasingly. A high tribute for any hymn!

Besides a change in lighting effect to heighten the joy of sacred music, he injects variety into the church music in other ways. He is music instructor, too, in one of the Portland high schools, and occasionally he invites a group of his best singers there to render sacred numbers in the evening church service, before the sermon. And the church has prospered and drawn large crowds, partly because of the ministry of music here, in addition to the excellent preaching. Both the main auditorium and the galleries are usually crowded.

One night recently, when the regular pastor was away in the East attending a conference, an evening of special music was planned, an evening when favorites and special request numbers were featured. The occasion was so delightful, attendants of the church are talking about it yet.

Professor Hollensted uses many devices to help increase interest in the hymns sung. Not long ago, just before the choir rendered a very lovely anthem about the sea, he explained how it came to be written; and, although the choir alone sang the anthem, the audience felt as if they, too, were participating because of their special interest in the message of the song. There was a certain *oneness* with the choral group and themselves, which would not have existed but for the talk given in advance.

A few Sundays ago the audience thrilled at viewing fresh and beautiful gowns worn by the choir. The choir members admitted that their old black gowns had been worn so long they fairly hated to put them on. But now the deep red gowns with white surplices help make God's house beautiful and help the church-goers to enjoy the music more. Variety and beauty do help the ministry of music. As one leader said, "Let's freshen up! We can serve better."

## Chapter III

# SINGING IN THE SPIRIT AND WITH THE UNDERSTANDING

Not only skill, but sincerity and understanding are essential if church music is to succeed. And when a congregation truly sings, it is not like putting on musical robes. The people sing because they are so full of the Holy Spirit they *must* give expression to their feelings. The power is from within.

I am thinking now of the late Mr. P. A. Ten Haaf, a Portland, Ore., chorister of unusual skill, insight, and understanding. When asked to voice his views on choir-directing-in-general, he replied that, "The function of a choir leader is not merely to wave a baton and 'choir-lead' in an ordinary, colorless fashion. Instead, the problem of the *real* choir leader is to instill into the choir and congregation a tone which *means* something. Proper tone and voice placement are of prime importance, and the lack of these is what constitutes grave criticism in the case of at least one symphony orchestra leader's ability whose instrumental work is above reproach."

Mr. Ten Haaf had, just prior to our interview, been acting as judge at a state-wide choral contest, he said; and, unfortunately, he had found many of the voices "blatant." Supplementing this statement, he, for example, sounded *"o."* First he uttered the vowel with his head only; then afterward with all his being vibrating with the fullness of the tone. "When songs are sung properly the whole body becomes a sounding-board for the voice," he explained. "And when a leader directs a choir or a congregation in singing, it's not simply from the soul of the leader to the voice of the singers,—it's *'from soul to soul'* if the meaningful tone is to be brought out in song."

Under Mr. Ten Haaf's able leadership I heard the congregation sing, "Rescue the Perishing." It was done with rich meaning and interest. This hymn, so often sung in a choppy manner that it is disliked by some, became effective and beautiful with the fine tones and the variety in expression from swelling sounds to soft, especially in the chorus. In "It is well with my soul" the spiritual message was effectively brought out by this great leader "under the Lord's direction." The early lines of the verses were soft, but when it came to, *"The trump shall resound,"* the congregation was lifted "almost to Heaven," with the greatly increased volume of sound.

One of the well-known, old-time hymns was made new by this choir leader's asking all the men in the congregation to stand and sing it alone. "And give them *all the organ you've got,"* he instructed the organist. The hymn was sung with rich tones and such feeling that both participants and hearers felt wonderfully blest. The women were invited to "all join in" on the last chorus, and the beautiful edifice fairly resounded with heavenly melody.

About the time of choir leader Ten Haaf's coming to White Temple, the evening service became somewhat less formal; and, after the numbers listed in the church bulletin were sung during the song-service, the pastor, Dr. William G. Everson, asked if anyone had a selection. Several had, and the friendly informality gave one sort of an old-fashioned "Sunday evening around-the-organ at home" feeling. The pastor made the music part of the service blend in well with the spoken word. After the "We ask it in Jesus' name" the organ and chimes closed with, "Jesus, the Very Thought of Thee" lines, which helped the congregation more truly to experience God.

The sermon itself, on the evening in question, was built around the Negro Spiritual, "Walking All Over God's Heaven." Dr. Everson said he once heard a Negro choir sing this number as he'd never heard it before. The choir members—many of them—worked in a neighborhood of wealthy white folks whose custom it was to wear a gown two or three times to society functions and then to give it to the colored servant. In this choir, therefore, all members of the group were resplendent: every man adorned in full dress suit, and every woman attractive in an evening gown. Some way he felt that all this magnificence possibly added to the feeling of exultation as the simple, well-loved Negro songs were sung in God's House in the "true southern spirit."

And Dr. Everson declared that when he selected his sermon subject, "Heaven," he could just hear that choir again as the chimes rang with "Walking all over God's Heaven." Incidentally, he explained that the message of the song embodied in the sentiment contained his own idea of

Heaven,—Heaven, not a place to sit around doing nothing for all eternity, but a place where its citizens were given work to do—in the furthering of God's Kingdom.

## CHAPTER IV

# THE POWER OF SACRED SONG

### By FLORA E. BRECK

*(This article originally appeared in the magazine,* THE CHOIR LEADER, *published by Lorenz.)*

Sometimes one is impressed anew with the wonderful power of sacred music for helping hearers to find the Lord. Occasionally even the *spoken* word (in sermons) has proved to be not quite so effective as is singing—when the singers have consecrated their talents to God. Recently we heard of how the ministry of music brought unexpected joy to a young man—and his wife and children were later made aware, in the home, of his changed heart.

The young man referred to—I will call him Jack, but that is not his name—had once been a church member, and had sung often in the choir;

but the war came, and all that was changed. For over a year he had been stationed in an especially unfavored place. It was not a combat area, but there was continual "battle" along three lines: against cold, monotony, and loneliness. While he did not noticeably wander so far away from God as some, yet he seemed to have lost touch with God, both then and upon his return home after the war.

He went to church occasionally, but then only to please his wife. His face was not alight with the joy of Christianity. Of course, there were many problems, too, in getting adjusted to civilian life. Then, one Sunday evening, he was feeling greatly dissatisfied with his condition. Often, in previous weeks he had heard the call, but had hardened himself against it. On this Sunday evening, the minister had spoken, but he had not responded. Then the visiting choir of college young people, who were participating in the service, sang an especially moving hymn. The music appealed. Quickly he handed over his sleeping young son to his wife. Erect, and with white-faced determination, he walked unhesitatingly down the aisle when the invitation was given.

"I felt it was now or never," he explained to his wife afterwards. "It was the singing of those young people that led me down the aisle," he thankfully explained. "Long months *I* had *wanted* to sing. In fact, the minister had asked me to sing in the quartet, but I felt it would be insincere. I smoked almost incessantly. The preacher didn't know that, nor how far away I felt I was from God. Much as I wished to accept the invitation to sing, I simply couldn't in that state."

Then while he was down at the altar the minister asked him if he had a further word of testimony. Jack finally explained that it was the message in the song of those young people (one of them a cripple) which helped him decide to accept salvation. Then and there, too, he confessed aloud how he had longed to sing but had been constrained by his own conscience. The minister's eyes were misty. "You *shall* sing again!" he said.

Some in the church had been praying, they had known of Jack's struggle, and they were moved by the young man's experience. The leaders rejoiced, too, that the special group of young people had "happened" to come that night to sing, for Jack went on to explain that it was just the singing of those young folks that brought him to the foot of the Cross.

We wonder if some pastors and choir committees realize what an inspiring thing it is to have a visiting choir of spiritual singers participate in the service occasionally. One can scarcely estimate the power of beautiful, spiritual singing in a praying church!

## Chapter V

# A FIVE-CHOIR CHURCH

### By Flora E. Breck

*(This article originally appeared in the magazine,* The Choir Leader, *published by Lorenz.)*

Music is of major importance in the services of the First Presbyterian Church of Portland, Oregon. Several years ago Mr. Clarence L. Faris was appointed Minister of Music, and a revival of interest in the music of this church dates from that time. Previous to his coming there had been a quartet instead of a chorus choir; and though the four voices were excellent, the coming of the larger choir has resulted in an increased interest in the musical part of the church services.

Forty-two men and women comprised the A Capella Choir there when first organized. From that beginning there have developed five choirs in the First Presbyterian Church: the A Capella Choir, the Adult Choir, the San Grael Choir (consisting of business people), the Junior Choir, and the Youth Choir. The A Capella Choir meets twice each week for rehearsals; the others once a week.

The A Capella was one of the first choirs of this type to be organized in the Northwest. Before being eligible for membership in this group, the singers must have appeared in concert work. Singing without an accompanying instrument naturally demands special skill in tone production; and Mr. Faris says there has been a demand for a new approach to voice teaching as a result of the organization of this choir. He feels that the developing of tones pleasing to hear is worth the expenditure of much time and effort.

A few minutes before the beginning and before the close of the regular choir rehearsals are devoted by this choir leader to hearing individuals sing alone briefly. One of the newer choir members confided to me that this method is not only improving her voice, but helps instill confidence in those not so sure of themselves.

All of the choirs wear vestments—robes of dull mahogany with cream surplices over the robes. By the way, the merchant who dyed the material for the robes experimented many times with color harmonies, with the result that the tone of the robes harmonizes perfectly with that of the wood-work of the church. The beauty and harmony of the physical surroundings, in fact, contribute much to the worshipful atmosphere that always prevails in the services there.

This choir leader conducts without a baton, indicating with his "sensitive, eloquent hands" the degrees of tone volume or expression.

Mr. Faris is particularly interested in children, and he believes it important to enlist their interest in the musical activities of the church. "It is a simple thing to organize a children's choir," he says. "The future of the church music depends on the children, and we must emphasize this part of the work. It is not difficult to interest children in church music. If only more parents might realize the value of this, many more children would be encouraged to join junior choirs. If the children become really interested in this project it is not difficult to keep their interest in choral work through high school and college years. For some young people an interest in choral work is a strong link in holding them to church loyalty during the years when many drift away from church attendance."

This song conductor believes there is a gain in having children sing without music in front of

35

them, memorizing the selections they sing. He feels that in this way he can get a more satisfactory tone production and musical expression. For some children the use of notes seems somewhat artificial,—a hindrance to free tone production.

Mr. Faris has heard most of the boy choirs in Europe, and says that many of them have a "hooty" quality to their singing. He believes that children can be trained to use clear, unstrained voices in singing. He adds that in training children to sing it is important to remind them frequently to maintain a straight posture instead of slumping over. Attention to this point adds much to the effectiveness of the singing.

When the First Presbyterian Junior Choir was organized there were almost forty-five youngsters from eight to twelve years of age. The director's wife, Mrs. Virginia Weber Faris, was conductor. At the dedicatory service of this Junior Choir they sang during the morning church service, being reinforced with four members of the adult A Capella Choir. All the music was sung from memory. Their voices were sweet, their behavior dignified, as they sang the anthem and responses effectively.

Regarding the directing of adult choirs, Mr.

Faris says: "Today there is no place for temperamental musicians. A group of singers must be a level-headed organization. A choir director should always be considerate of the feelings of his singers. Rehearsals should be carefully prepared for. The choir members should realize that the music is a very important part of the church service, and that it should have as much care in preparation as the pastor gives to the sermon."

Asked if he always selected hymns and anthems with special reference to the subject of the sermon, Mr. Faris replied in the negative. Yet the musical part of the First Church services is often closely related to the thought of the sermon. His intention is to plan the music in such a way that it not only constitutes an integral part of the church services as a whole, but is a worship unit in itself.

I asked one of the choir members what in her estimation Mr. Faris stressed most in choral work. She replied that, in practicing on "special occasion numbers," such as Christmas services, etc., he tried to get away from the old English style of singing, the chanting, monotonous type, and strove to make the lines lead up to a point of strong interest—a climax.

Variety should characterize the musical part of

the church services, this expert music leader emphasizes. Sometimes the choir may sing without accompaniment, sometimes with the organ. On certain occasions an anthem may follow the "long prayer," on others the special music should come earlier in the service. A variety of prayer responses is used by Mr. Faris.

Interest was added to the musical part of the church program when the San Grael Choir sang the first and last verse of one of the hymns from the front choir-loft, the middle verse being rendered by the Adult Choir in the gallery in the rear of the church, the singing by the latter group being softer in tone than the other. The illusion of distance was artistic and delightful.

An event of special interest to Portland music lovers was the production of Stainer's "Crucifixion," one Good Friday. This was given by the combined choirs of the First Presbyterian Church. The large auditorium was filled to capacity, and the oratorio was sung with deeply moving effect.

Church attendants at the First Presbyterian notice especially how carefully every detail of the services is planned. The church bulletin, for instance, carries a note to the ushers to seat latecomers only at points in the service indicated by stars on the calendar. In this way beautiful responses, etc., are not rudely broken into by a stirring of stragglers up the aisle, and the system serves to ease nerve-strain for both song-leader and pastor.

To go back for a moment to choir-cooperation, good fellowship prevails to an unusual degree among the members. Separate socials are frequently held for the different choir groups, and occasionally inter-choir social affairs are planned.

The ministry of music has been a large factor in building up the interest of the large congregations that attend the First Church. In particular, the large attendance at the evening services is worthy of mention. While some churches have had to discontinue their evening services, and many others have small numbers in attendance, at this church there are always upwards of three hundred in the evening, and happily a large proportion of them are young people.

## Chapter VI

## A LETTER FROM A WASHINGTON CHOIR MEMBER

I asked a Washington, D.C. choir member to jot down some of her ideas as to choir matters for including in this book, but she was busy and kept deferring it. Finally she covered several pages with an apology that her thoughts weren't organized at all, and told me to "sort 'em out." But I felt her suggestions would be helpful without polishing or rearranging them, so they are offered here. All she asked was that I would not include her name to the "scattered thoughts." Here is her letter:

First, I want to talk about the *selection of music* to be used by the choir. A varied program should be provided, as there is a wide difference in the musical tastes and preferences of people. The publishers' lists include a great many beautiful anthems which are not too difficult for the average choir to sing well; and the careful selection of suitable pieces is well worth the expenditure of much time and prayerful thought.

One important point to remember is to avoid the use of anthems which are beyond the ability of the choir members to sing well. A simple hymn sung effectively is infinitely to be preferred to a difficult anthem haltingly performed. No matter how much rehearsing is done, a choir cannot give a satisfying rendering of music which is beyond their ability. The faltering performance of music which is too difficult is a disappointing experience for both the choir and the congregation.

Another important point to keep in mind is the need of avoiding the too frequent use of some one particular type of music just because the director happens to have a special fondness for it. I know of one instance in which the leader majored on Bach chorales for many weeks in succession, with the result that many in the congregation and a majority of the choir members acquired a definite prejudice against music composed by Bach. It is desirable for every choir to include an occasional Bach selection in the program of music selected; but the ability to appreciate much of the music composed by Bach requires more of a background of musical education than is possessed by most people, and it is therefore not a good idea for the average choir to include Bach music too frequently. There are so very many selections to choose from which will evoke the enthusiasm of both singers and audience that there is no excuse for using anthems which are not rewarding for the time spent in rehearsing them.

While it is essential to avoid choosing music that is

too difficult for the choir members concerned to use in the church service, it is excellent training for the choir group to spend *part* of the time at every rehearsal in practicing music which is recognized by all as beyond their present ability to sing in public but which they will greatly enjoy attempting for their own satisfaction when no audience is present to notice inadequacies. Such practice adds greatly to the interest and enthusiasm of the members of the choir, and is fine training for them. Eight or nine years ago, our own church choir did this. We found to our surprise that a year or so after we had tried out relatively difficult numbers just to see what we could do with them, enough improvement had been made in the ability of the group as a whole that we sang with confidence and really pleasing effect numbers which at first were far beyond our ability to sing in public,— some of those numbers which we first tried only as practice material were used later in church services and apparently enjoyed by everybody. Our choir still does this occasionally, though not as much as previously.

Then, regarding *keeping the choir rehearsals on a businesslike basis* so far as promptness in starting and closing are concerned, and also regarding the importance of not wasting time on trivialities,—I could write considerable! A rehearsal which is scheduled to start at eight o'clock and to close at quarter past nine should hold strictly to those hours. For a person who works through the day and comes home tired, it is a very annoying experience to go to choir practice at the announced hour for starting, and find only three or four people present, and then wait around for twenty minutes before the rehearsal gets under way. It is almost as annoying, also, to start late the next time because of the experience of waiting for others to arrive on previous occasions, only to find that for once the rehearsal has started promptly, and that the first one or two numbers have been missed because of counting on a late start. If the habit of promptness is established and strictly maintained, the members will respond by arriving promptly.

And, as a related matter, I feel like including a few lines about the importance of sticking closely to business during the rehearsal, and not taking time out in the middle of the session to discuss plans for the next picnic, or a shower for John and Mary who expect to be married next month. Those who want to visit with each other can have their informal session for as long as they wish after the rehearsal is over, but—for pity's sake—let's don't fritter away the time of busy, tired members who greatly enjoy the singing, but who wish when the rehearsal is over to have a chance to get back home and get a bath and go to bed!

Maybe you won't like this idea, but somewhere in a book of this type there might be opportunity to bring in the necessity of planning in such a way that the choir will be safeguarded from the inclusion of people who really don't have *any* singing capacity. Monotones are exceptional, but every once in a while a monotone appears who likes music and thinks it would be nice to join the choir. The other choir members should be protected from such. Six years or more ago I sat next to a mono-tone for three or four months. She was a dear girl, but it was terrible to try to read music against her at-tempted singing which was always off-key and definitely in the monotone class. It was a real relief when she married and moved to another part of the city—much as I enjoyed her society when we weren't trying to sing together. It is a fairly frequent practice to issue a general invitation to all and sundry to join the choir and help the music. Probably more than ninety per cent of those who respond to such a general invitation would be welcome additions to a volunteer choir. But the exclusion of a definitely impossible candidate could be accomplished without too much difficulty by announcing that those who are interested to join the choir are in-vited to consult with the leader at such and such a time and place. This would give an opportunity to screen out the hopeless ones without too much loss of face.

But I mustn't end this paper on such a sour note. The most important of the *general thoughts* I have concern-ing choirs is that a well conducted choir constitutes an opportunity for a deeply spiritual experience for the members, if the music is chosen with good judgment. Many of the numbers rehearsed and sung in public deal with Christian experience in a very personal way. When a selection of special beauty and depth of meaning is sung in the church service, the *audience* hears it *once*, and it may not make a very great impression unless special circumstances are such as to make that particular theme significant and helpful to certain individuals. But before the *choir* sings the selection, it is rehearsed repeatedly; and if the theme is a deeply spiritual one, it can be a very moving experience *for the participants*. For instance, when I mentioned to a friend the other day that I had regretfully decided to give up the choir temporarily because of other church work, she said she was really sorry to hear it, for she knew how much it meant to me. She told me that years ago, in Cleveland, before she came to Washington, she belonged to the choir in the church which she attended. She said that one year for the Christmas program the choir sang part of the oratorio, "The Messiah," and that as they rehearsed the portions which refer to the passion of Christ—in particular the parts including, "He was wounded for our transgressions" and "Surely He hath borne our griefs and carried our sorrows"—she just felt as if she had been converted all over again. That type of experience in rehearsing the best type of choir music is not exceptional, I am sure. It makes me wish that more of the Christians musically qualified knew how choir members *themselves* are blest in participating in group singing of this kind.

## Chapter VII

# EACH ESTEEMING THE OTHER BETTER THAN HIMSELF

### By FLORA E. BRECK

*(This article originally appeared in the magazine, THE CHOIR LEADER, published by Lorenz.)*

Musicians sometimes show the quality of their Christianity as much by their dealings with their fellow-men as by their singing. It is fine that choir members enjoy singing, but there are occasional times when it is the generous and Christian thing to restrain one's eagerness in favor of others.

A visiting minister recently described a situation that he had witnessed which would have been really ludicrous if it had not been so unlovely and un-Christian. There had been divided responsibility for some weeks between two organists, and at an impressively large evening service both young women were bent on being organist for the evening. Each had come in at a different entrance of the church, but at about the same time. Each saw the other, and each accelerated her footsteps more and more, as the other was manifestly going to reach the instrument first. One of them "made it" just a hair's breadth ahead of the other. One was triumphant, the other indignant, and the feeling of each was so plainly written on the countenance that the worship spirit in the congregation was broken. The entire service was marred by the occurrence.

A music leader, if he be of the highest type, can do much to alleviate tense situations, and prevent embarrassing moments. Blessed are the song leaders who are themselves so spiritual that they just naturally imbue the choir members with the importance of the injunction, "Let us sing unto the *Lord!*" I once visited a choir rehearsal, and the leader frankly talked over a certain difficult situation which was bound to occur the following Sunday. "I know we shall all get along just fine," he said, "for we are all *Christians,* you know!" And they did.

All of us have been impressed at times while watching and listening to a choir of the highest type. The light of sincerity is beautiful to witness. We feel it is a recommendation of the Gospel professed. To be able to worship and get along in a true humility with other members of a choral group is a fine achievement. I am thinking now of a circumstance I had occasion to know about in our own city, some time ago.

Mr. Z. had been asked by the quartet leader to join the quartet, because of his unusually good voice. It was understood that an older member of the group was withdrawing because of pressure of outside duties. Mr. Z. was, to use his own expression, "all steamed up" at the opportunity offered him. He had taken such a part in another city, and had greatly enjoyed the singing. So he rehearsed that week at the appointed time, though he had to drive twenty miles to do so. In fact, every morning of the week and while at work his appointment to sing was uppermost in his mind. Usually when Sunday mornings came, his family would have to urge him to get up, but this time he was up early, practicing his part, and getting the rest of the family up. His heart sang as he thought of the evening service with its opportunity for participating in the ministry of music.

No one ever knows exactly how such things happen, nor whose fault it is, but that evening there was a mix-up. In some way the retiring member of the quartet arrived early, and Mr. Z.

came in just on time. The latter looked up front. There was already the full quota of quartet members. His heart sank. He couldn't understand it, for had *he* not been asked? The light went out of his face. All during the service he felt dumbfounded, though he sang the congregational numbers. He wondered what the explanation could be. It finally developed that there had been a case of divided responsibility between the pastor and the song-leader. The song-leader thought he was to appoint a new member; the minister heard that the one who was to leave was staying on, and he felt it was quite all right.

Although Mr. Z. was inexpressibly disappointed, he did not let this interfere with his church attendance or with his hearty participation in the congregational singing. In fact, he even accommodated in connection with serving the quartet! He accidentally learned that one of the members of the quartet lived near him. The latter's car was out of order, and on the "night of the big snow" there was no means of transportation to choir practice. Mr. Z. heard of it. He forthwith took his own car and transported this neighbor member to the rehearsal. This gracious service was more than appreciated, for the other quartet members heard of the deed, and were greatly impressed by the attitude displayed by the "let out" member. "That's really going the second mile!" one said to another.

Not only did Mr. Z. transport his friend. He did more. He sat back listening, and noticed that one member was singing while standing at a tangent to the others. There was no "oneness." When there was a pause in the rehearsal, Mr. Z. mentioned he had recently heard a famous quartet, and he explained that one way the marvelous harmony was achieved was by the four getting their heads and their shoulders closer together. The church group listened, and tried out his suggestion. The improvement was a revelation to them. "I am so glad you made that suggestion," said one afterwards. "It made all the difference in the world." As Mr. Z. had sat and watched the change in posture of the four, his own face was alight, and his whole body was in tune with them. Even though circumstances were not such that he could be one of them at that time, his enthusiasm kindled their own, and the singing was more alive. One of the most spiritual members of the quartet explained later to me that it was amazing the way a depressing inadvertence had worked out in the case of Mr. Z. The Christian spirit triumphed, and the outcome of the incident was such that the angels in Heaven must have rejoiced to behold them.

If this would-be quartet member had displayed a resentful spirit about the whole affair, it would have been a tragedy instead of a blessing. An elderly woman who chanced to hear of the incident spoke appreciatively to the singer in question, but he made light of what he had done, explaining how his mother used to emphasize to him, when he felt he had been humiliated, this thought: "In quietness shall be your strength." He said he had never forgotten what she had said.

"And so I feel that it doesn't always pay to 'stand up for my rights—regardless,'" he smiled.

The little elderly lady to whom he was talking responded, quoting Philippians 2:3,

"Let nothing be done through strife or vainglory; but in lowliness of mind let each esteem other better than themselves."

And she added, "You have shown us that this pays—in a wonderful way!"

## Chapter VIII

# WHEN USHERING IN A NEW ORDER OF SERVICE

When ushering in a new season, or a new series of sermons, or a new plan for music, or a new choir director—it seems well to institute the newness with *emphasis* and with especially well-prepared worship services. By following this plan the members of the congregation are in an anticipatory mood and eager to attend because variety adds richness.

For instance, when Max D. Risinger was recently installed Director of Music at the First Baptist Church in Portland, Ore., it was a memorable—and blessed—occasion. A feeling of fresh inspiration pervaded the meeting—even to the gleaming white surplice effects and deep red gowns which the choir wore.

The pastor and choir leader integrated the theme of the evening service perfectly, namely, the truth of Christ's coming to seek and save those who are lost, as exemplified by the Lost

Sheep and the thoughts contained in the Twenty-third Psalm.

In some churches there is not a large percentage of men, but at this church ("White Temple," it is called) men take a deep and abiding interest in the Work, and one of the highlights of this occasion was a Men's Chorus (of thirty-some members) which came to the platform, standing in front of the vested choir. The Men's Choir sang with the regular choir, "The Ninety and Nine" by Sankey. The second verse one of the men sang as a solo, with humming accompaniment by all the others on the platform. It was so appreciated that some wondered why it couldn't be done "this way oftener." The rendition of this famous and well-loved hymn was stirring; and when the entire choral group took up the lines including "thunder-riven," and "Rejoice, for the Lord brings back His own," the congregation seemed lifted "almost to Heaven," so exultant was the singing. During the evening the leader gave a brief account of how Sankey came to compose this hymn extemporaneously. (If interested, please go to the Music Room of your Public Library.)

The supplementary Men's Choir—with the enthusiasm engendered—seemed to produce a feeling of *oneness* with the vested choir and with the congregation in general; and later in the evening the pastor announced what night of the forthcoming week this group would rehearse. He emphasized that it was not merely for a chosen few men, this old-time Gospel-hymn singing. *"Every* man of this congregation is invited to join this group," he reiterated. This enlarged men's organization bids fair to become an important factor in adding to the beauty and helpfulness of the worship service, as well as in stimulating the attendance.

To help honor the new Minister of Music, there was a reception for Mr. and Mrs. Risinger in the new addition of the building afterwards. There were musical numbers on the program, and flowers were pinned on the new-comers.

But, to go back to the main church service, among the Shepherd-theme music selections of the evening, the following were included: "The King of Love My Shepherd Is" (anthem); "The Ninety and Nine" by Campion (a tenor solo); the invitation hymn, "Where He Leads" (by choir and congregation); and Virginia Walker, daughter of the pastor, Dr. Ralph Walker, sang as a solo, "He Shall Feed His Flock." Naturally, the sermon topic was, "The Ninety and Nine," with Matthew and Luke references being read. After the closing prayer the choir sang the beautiful response, "Hear Our Prayer, O God. . . ."

All-in-all, the service was one which tended to draw Christians nearer to God, and non-Christians to the Good Shepherd Who came to seek and to save the lost.

## Chapter IX

# FEATURING HYMN-ANTHEMS

### By Flora E. Breck

(*This article originally appeared in the magazine,* The Choir Leader, *published by Lorenz.*)

Congregations enjoy helping to plan the evening church worship services which they attend. Thus figured Waldemar H. Hollensted, Director of Music at the First Baptist Church of Portland, Oregon. He seems to find there is more of a *oneness* between choir and congregation when the latter is permitted to have some voice in the selections to be used. So he is now giving the audience opportunity to request numbers for the hymn-anthem part of the music included. This, of course, refers to the evening service.

"Softly and Tenderly" was one of the first selected by a member of the congregation for a hymn-anthem number. The singing by the choir was simple, effective, and greatly loved. And the congregation is eagerly looking forward to the coming months when more of these specially requested hymn-anthems will be used.

In singing these, certain lines of the hymn are sung as solos, others as duets, quartets, etc., as seems appropriate; and, of course, considerable of the hymn-anthem consists of singing by the large chorus choir. Even though the congregation is not doing the singing, it has a special feeling that "this is *our* service," since the selecting orginates in the pew.

Professor Hollensted, who is also Glee Club Director in Jefferson High School in Portland, believes much can be done in the cause of better music in churches which will brighten up choir programs. He declares, "There is so much that can be done, but the music profession is so steeped in tradition and inhibitions that many are afraid to branch away from the stereotyped way of doing things. 'We must do it this way because it always has been done this way,' seems to be the thought, and so the audience goes away at times unstimulated, just as though the preacher were to give the same sermon every Sunday."

Always there is stately dignity and beauty in the worship services here in the First Baptist Church, and yet there is sufficient variety to appeal to both old and young, so that the ministry of music really lifts.

In having the hymn-anthems which are being included now, the church attendants who enjoy simple hymns more than the more formal choral anthems, feel that their wishes are being respected in a distinctive way; yet those who prefer the regular type of anthem find that they also are being remembered, for there is also a regular anthem rendered during each evening service.

## Chapter X

# AFTER-SERVICE HYMN-SINGS

## *By* Flora E. Breck

(*This article originally appeared in the maga-zine,* The Choir Leader, *published by Lorenz.*)

The after-evening-service "hymn-sing" in-cluded at the First Baptist Church of Portland, Ore., each Sunday night is proving a delightful feature, and its by-products are many. When Dr. Ralph Walker first came to serve as pastor of this large church a few months ago, he explained to the congregation that in a former pastorate in Ohio the informal gospel song services held there each Sunday evening, after the regular preach-ing service, had been found one of the most inter-esting and important parts of his work there, and would they like to have him inaugurate a similar feature in this new field in Portland? They would. And from the start an enormous congre-gation stayed for these "hymn-sings," for they seem to have a function and a flavor which supplement admirably the more formal preaching service.

Directly after the benediction the "magic doors," to the wing of the church, part, and almost immediately the pianist starts off with a well-loved old-time gospel hymn, which puts the gathering crowd into good humor, for some admittedly never do get their fill of hymn-singing in any preaching service.

The pastor himself is leader in these song-services, and the singing starts whole-heartedly. Some Sundays there is a mimeographed sheet given to each member of the audience, and the page contains five or six well-known gospel hymns—the words only—on which the copyright has expired. And how the congregations love to sing them!

Variety in conducting this unique service adds to its interest. Sometimes there is a talented young woman trumpet-player who plays a verse of a hymn while all join in the chorus. Sometimes someone who sings especially well in the audience is invited to sing alone. Sometimes a service man, just passing through Portland, lends his musical ability. Occasionally an elderly person of good voice—or a very young person—sings special numbers. And everyone has an enormously good time. Even the galleries are usually filled.

More and more, it seems, music is being considered, not a thing apart from life, but an integral part of daily living. Neighborliness, too, is injected into these services in a genuinely delightful way after the congregation has sung a lot of old-time favorites. Then it is that Doctor Walker is wont to say, "Now I would like to ask a favor. Will all those who have never been in this church before please stand up." They do. "And now this is easier yet: Will all those who are standing please come to the front of the room." A goodly crowd good-naturedly follows suit. "And now, this is the easiest of all: I wish each one of you would tell me your name, where you are from—and if you will, we would be so glad to have you give us a word of testimony—not over a minute or two."

Then the pastor interrogates each in such a friendly, informal way that those who might ordinarily feel shy have no such embarrassment here. The minister stands down from the platform facing them, so each feels about as free to reply as though alone in the pastor's study, for the "ice is decidedly broken!"

Many a time there are missionaries in the visiting lineup, sometimes a soldier or a sailor, young folks, old, and even high school students. Many of the testimonies given are a real spiritual blessing. And the pastor is genuinely interested in the name of each individual. If he doesn't hear it he will ask that it be repeated. Often he will know their own pastor, and all proceed to feel at home. In fact, the time passes so pleasantly that the intended "twenty minutes or so" sometimes means almost 10 p.m. "Sing Them Over Again to Me," "Abide with Me," "God Bless America," etc., are inspiringly and helpfully sung. Accessions in membership come, and sociability is increased as these people sing with joy the old gospel hymns. This "hymn-sing" feature is "one of the nicest things in the church," attendants say.

## Chapter XI

# CHURCH NOTICES FURTHER CHOIR INTERESTS

The interests of the choir can be furthered to a considerable extent when there is close cooperation between the choir leader or choir secretary and the one who prepares the church bulletin each week. When additional members are being recruited for the choir and when new choirs of different age-groups are being organized, a note to that effect in the church calendar is likely to prove effective, along with an invitation to confer with the choir leader.

The First Presbyterian Church of Portland, Ore., well-known for the sweetness and beauty—and worshipfulness—of its ministry of music, included one of the loveliest announcements and welcomes imaginable to the choir the first Sunday in September one year. The paragraph is quoted below:

"AGAIN WE WELCOME THE CHOIR AND MR. EVANS. Theirs is a ministry in worship to which they are called and prepared by the grace and gifts of God. Music is not of men, but through men. The Divine Artist is the Master Composer. But it has pleased Him to bestow upon some persons the gift of catching and expressing the silent harmonies of the universe. Thus comes song. By it our hearts are lifted in praise to the giver of every good and perfect gift. We wish them joy in their work, and thank them for the service they render us in common worship of God. Mr. Evans will be glad to confer with any persons who wish to enlist for this service."

John Stark Evans is organist and choirmaster of this church. He also has charge of the music department in one of the colleges in Portland. Recently he gave an address on "Church Music" to a church group in this city. Dr. Paul S. Wright is minister of First Presbyterian in Portland, and the close cooperation between these two leaders means unusually helpful worship services for attendants.

But no matter how skillfully the choir and choir leader serve, they are human, and a word of appreciation strengthens and encourages. A paragraph in the church calendar helps, but if you, a hearer, have been blest by the singing of a certain hymn, won't you tell them so. An expression of your feelings will be more gratefully received than you can imagine. Such appreciation, too, will be a guide in selecting future songs.

And be sure to use the church bulletin for announcement of forthcoming special choral offerings of music. The inclusion of such notices several weeks in advance will help build up interest and attendance. Of course, too, the music committee will see that adequate publicity of such events is secured through the daily *newspapers*. *Secular* musical events usually get wide publicity, and religious leaders also are becoming increasingly aware of the value of the printed word in arousing interest in *sacred* concerts. Aim to assign someone to handle your choir notices who is an experienced writer and one who gets things done on time. It will pay.

CHAPTER XII

# VISITING GROUPS OUTSIDE
# THE CHURCH

For church choirs to confine their singing activities to church music programs is something like keeping one's religious life for use on Sundays only. Today we hear of more and more choir directors planning definitely to expand their usefulness by "extracurricular" activities and programs. Many people never enter a church—either because of lack of interest, lack of time, or lack of opportunity. Progressive choir leaders who have broad vision encourage their groups to extend their ministry of song to other audiences by making occasional visits to homes for the aged, hospitals, prisons, broadcasting studios, etc.

I recently received a letter from my sister, who is a member of one of the church choirs, in Washington, D.C., in which she wrote of such a visit, as follows: "Yesterday afternoon our choir went out to Blue Plains (the District poorhouse) for an hour of music. We went through the several sitting rooms singing such hymns as *Blessed Assurance, The Old Rugged Cross, He Leadeth Me, Shall We Gather at the River?* In this visit we included the hospital wards where the bed patients are housed. It was a saddening experience to see how pathetic many of the guests appeared, but it was very heart-warming to see how responsive and appreciative they were of our coming. In the rooms where the colored people were housed, many of them joined in the singing,—more of them than of the white people.

"Last year we made a similar visit, and regretted that we had not brought refreshments with us. This year we brought many pounds of cookies, donated by members of the choir and friends who knew where we were going. There must have been over a thousand cookies in all— which was not so many as it sounds, as there are nearly 500 men and women housed at Blue Plains."

Homer Rodeheaver, world-famous Gospel song leader, has done a great deal to bring a *joyous* Christianity, through music, to the "far corners" of the world. And I am sure he would tell you that he, also, has found a blessing in this ministry. In his travels, he sang often to underprivileged groups in many places. In the course of studying the history of Negro spirituals, he learned from his Negro friends that many of these songs were *"born"* rather than composed. These spirituals sprang, he said, out of the hardships of life where these people were placed, for they had special need for spiritual resources and up-look to the *Heavenly* Home because of their dire poverty and suffering *here*.

Taking choral music to hospitals is one of the most appreciated of church ministries. Not only is this a medium for introducing Christ to hungry hearts, but doctors and nurses find that in many instances sweet singing has definite therapeutic value. Anxious spirits and troubled minds are calmed, and bodily pain is frequently eased by the strains of sacred music. Even some of the hospital attendants who are not themselves Christians admit that sacred song has definite healing power.

And who can estimate the value of church music which comes into homes, to those on highways, etc., over the *radio?* The choir music which many of the stations provide constitutes worship services which are a joy and blessing. Some of us thank the Lord every day for the *availability* of sacred song. A friend of mine, a great appreciator of church music, tells me that over every choral rendering there is a definite shadow: the knowledge that the strains will come to an *end* too soon!

It always seems to me that the sacred song singers who lend their voices in humble places— where music seldom is heard—make the Heavenly Hosts rejoice, as well as the individuals to whom they minister. Many hymns include Scriptural lines, so we don't need to *wonder* if the singing of them will be blest. We *know!*

Referring again to the subject of church choir members being willing to sing when the audience is small, or the listeners not those in high places, I was interested in a helpful little poem appearing several years ago in ALLIANCE WEEKLY. Here it is:

> "Father, where shall I work today?"
>   And my love flowed warm and free.
> Then He pointed me toward a tiny spot
>   And said, "Tend that for Me."
> I answered quickly, "Oh, no, not that,
>   Why no one would ever see,
> No matter how well my work was done,
>   In that little place for me."
> And the word He spoke, it was not stern,

He answered me tenderly:
"Ah, little one, search that heart of thine,
   Art thou working for them or Me?
Nazareth was a little place,
   And so was Galilee."

              (Author—Unknown)

## Chapter XIII

# HYMN-SINGS HELP PAY OFF MORTGAGE

## By Flora E. Breck

(*This article originally appeared in the magazine,* The Choir Leader, *published by Lorenz.*)

The writer received a letter from a friend in Connecticut telling how hymn-sings and choice flowers are helping to reduce the mortgage indebtedness on a parsonage. The hymn-sings were held in the homes of various of the church members. Of course there wasn't a charge for admission, but silver offerings were taken, and the amounts received in all were very considerable. Incidentally, these occasions helped in no small way to promote good feeling, for music has a habit of doing that. And it also fostered music *appreciation* among those who attended these get-togethers, for a good many who came admitted that they just "hadn't noticed the hymns much before." Interest in the hymns and the hymn-writers was increased by giving brief sketches of the life and work of some of the authors of the hymns used.

This is a music magazine, so possibly flowers shouldn't be "dragged in," but it may not be amiss to mention that one of the hymn-singers above mentioned, supplemented the money-raising by growing choice, named gladiolus bulbs in her yard. Very gorgeous and elegant gladiolus spikes developed, and when offered for sale they were snapped up quickly, both for their beauty and "for the good of the cause." That musical flower-grower netted exactly $60 during the summer from her floricultural endeavors, all of which went toward the parsonage mortgage fund.

And the choir members were reminded again that music is not a thing apart from life, but that it can be effectively blended with "hearts and flowers" in a way which makes for spiritual and material profit. From $1,560, the parsonage mortgage has now been reduced to $990, through the ministry of music and flowers.

## Chapter XIV

# ILLUSTRATED SONG SERVICE ATTRACTS

### By Flora E. Breck

*(This article originally appeared in the magazine, The Choir Leader, published by Lorenz.)*

(Editor's Note: We are printing Miss Breck's article because of whatever suggestive values it may have for our readers. It is not to be understood as an endorsement of the spectacular and theatrical features here reported, for reproduction in our church services. There are some things that a passing evangelist or evangelistic group may do with impunity that would be strongly resented if it were attempted by the resident pastor. In recent years the churches have given a large place to the dramatic presentation of truth, and we heartily welcome that. Nevertheless there are proprieties to be observed in our church services which, in our judgment, must relegate certain features off the church platform. Each, of course, must judge for himself as to what is fitting and what is not.

But there are suggestions in Miss Breck's report that

might prove to be quite helpful to other churches planning for programs that break away from the dead routine of things. The thought of building a song service around the pilot and stormy sea idea is a very practical one, as is also that of making the cross the conception around which the songs and remarks group themselves. It should be easy to find other possibilities of a similar nature. Such song services, or "sermons in song," are by no means a new experiment but have been tried out with much success for many years. Now for Miss Breck's story.)

Illustrated sermons were common enough, Miss Bernice Cobb of Portland, Oregon, figured; but an evening devoted to illustrated *songs*—that should be an idea worth trying, she decided. So one night the "Cobb Sisters," well-known Northwestern evangelistic singers, put on such a service in the large hall where their "Roberts-Cobb Revival Services" had continued for several weeks.

That night there was no regular sermon whatever, and this novel service was so much enjoyed that the audience insisted on an early repetition of the program. And the second night of illustrated songs drew a large house again, for certain variations of the original program had been announced.

The sermon-in-song was built around the "life-is-a-stormy-sea and Christ-the-Pilot" idea. All week long the evangelistic party had splashed paint on a huge canvas and manipulated hammers, nails and rocks, so that the platform was transformed into a "breaking-waves-dashed high" effect, with lowering sky and appropriate coastline of rocks. Happily, dim lights covered up objects which would otherwise spoil the illusion. But the attention centered mostly on a large lighthouse at the left which had been constructed with a door in it and a real beacon-light at the top, which shone, then went off, and on again periodically throughout the service. It was very realistic indeed.

The audience, too, was surprised and pleased to note how many sea and pilot hymns there are. "Throw out the Lifeline" came first, then "Jesus, Savior, Pilot Me," "The Haven of Rest," "Let the Lower Lights be Burning," "Drifting," "How Well I Know Who Pilots Me," "The Hand That Never Lets Go," "The Rock Holds Me," etc.

A certain two-part number was very beautiful indeed. It was entitled "Taps" and "Send the Light." The first part, a young soldier in uniform sounded "Taps," then "Send the Light" was sung by the choir. "Sail On" also was used as an instrumental number.

"Rock of Ages" was one of the most effective and helpful hymns sung, with lights low and the sky dark and threatening. During the "Drifting" song a real boat heaved in sight with several persons sitting in it, rowing carelessly over the make-believe sea. Doubtless a rope propelled the boat, but the effect was of the boat just drifting along the water across the platform.

The climax came when the two Cobb sisters in white flowing robes sang "Throw a Line," the rendition of which has made them famous in Portland and environs. At a number of places in the song they would manipulate a real rope, circle it above their heads to give it momentum before throwing it out to sea. An exhausted form was in the water struggling for his life. Finally he caught the line, and the boy was dragged to shore by these young women. Throughout the act thunder roared and lightning played over the black sea. It was wonderfully vivid, and thrilled the audience, for the hymn itself has a splendid swing.

This type of service, on the life-saving theme, was particularly heart-searching and timely, coming as it did just after the "Akron" disaster with its toll of victims and few survivors from the sea.

At the close of the service the audience and choir sang "Come into my heart, come into my heart, come into my heart, Lord Jesus," over and over again. It was a tender, beautiful closing to the evangelistic service; and hearts were won for the Kingdom.

The program was varied by instrumental numbers in between the choral selections. A gifted young man played his accordion delightfully. He is one of the most skillful artists in this line, having been picked up in a Western city by Doctor Roberts, leader of the evangelistic party, on one of the boy's theatrical coast-to-coast tours. The lad was converted and turned from a "vaudevillian" to a Christian-musician. One seldom hears such talent in a religious service except where a large wage is paid. The audience at the service was not slow to show appreciation, and the applause brought "Arney" back again and again.

So much interest was awakened in this illustrated-song type of evangelistic meeting that the Cobb sisters immediately planned an evening where the Cross was to be featured, electrically-lighted.

"The Old Rugged Cross" hymn was the principal song, besides "In the Cross of Christ I Glory," along with other kindred songs.

There is much rhythm injected into the sacred songs as led by the Cobb sisters, and the *tempo* is quicker than some listeners would admire, but certain it is their plan of music appeals to the masses. Crowds come for the singing, hear the message and become saved. These less-privileged souls are drawn to such meetings where they might never go near a more formal type of service. The Cobb sisters nearly always select the joyous type of songs.

These singers make much use of the radio for stimulating interest in their church services. One broadcast put on weekly Sunday nights from eleven to twelve calls forth a lot of interest.

## Chapter XV

# SECULAR CHOIR CONCERT SOLVES MONEY PROBLEM

*By* Flora E. Breck

*(This article originally appeared in the magazine,* The Choir Leader, *published by Lorenz.)*

When the Portland, Oregon, Rose City Community Church quartet burst forth into a large chorus choir the problem of providing wherewithal for the purchasing of choir music became a serious one. The quartet had been "let out" because of low church finances, and the choir director faced the "four-each" of many music selections in the choir cupboard with real dismay. Many of the pieces, too, were adapted only to a quartet choir.

But the enterprising new choir leader, Mr. Victor DePinto, conceived the idea of staging a church concert during a week-day evening, a "silver collection" affair. Inwardly he felt a little dubious about the size of audience such an event would draw during the winter season, but he went forward with faith, engaging some of the finest musical talent in Portland for the night late in February.

The choir decided that a small room well-filled would be better than a scattering audience in the fine new church auditorium. And so the rocking-chaired, fire-placed room was selected, the one where soft rugs and lights were delightful even without music. But to the joy of the director and choir, the audience was large, and a more appreciative one would be hard to find. The choir exchequer, too, was replenished, so the choir director didn't need to worry about music finances for some time to come.

But "almost more" than the money, the good fellowship created was worth while. This music fete revived new interest in fine music in that community. The program was barely an hour long, and appetites were whetted for another evening "just like that one." Following were among the numbers rendered:

Gypsy Life ...................... Scott
Now by Day's Retiring Lamp ...... Bishop
Caro Nome (Rigoletto) ............. Verdi
The Mocking Bird ................ Basset

80

Air .......................... Bach
Valentine's Aria (Faust) .......... Gounod
Litany ....................... Strauss
Break, Break, Break (Tennyson) ..... Tidy
Gaily in Our Boat We Row ........ Woolley
The Shoogy Shoe ............... Ambrose

Portland's famous blind singer, Miss Marguerite Carney, sang the third and fourth numbers with rare sweetness. The high liquid notes transported her hearers "nearly to heaven." Clear, simple singing it was. In fact, every selection on the program was exceptionally beautiful.

The choir members all wore their best, and the floral decorations up front were remindful of Valentine's Day with their redness. A line on the concert program as to the florist donor brought the flowers without charge.

And after the program, the choir and their friends repaired to the basement where the inner man was ministered to. That also cost the choir nothing, for oranges and lemons were salvaged from a recent church reception in the basement. And the dainty cookies served were an aftermath of a missionary luncheon of the day before. So "a good time was had by all," with very little expense and considerable profit.

Mr. DePinto was so new a leader that the church congregation had felt little acquainted with him prior to this event. Viewing only the back of him in the choir Sundays, black-suited, erect and highly dignified, led them to believe that he bore the solemnity of a funeral director; but the night of the concert they were surprised and pleased at his humanness. It seemed he had inadvertently left his handkerchief in the ante-room and he simply couldn't return immediately to retrieve it. Would one of the choir ladies lend him hers? She would. He eyed its diminutive laciness, but appropriated it, asking immediately for another lady's hankie to reinforce the first. It was forthcoming, but by this time the choir and front rows in the audience were convulsed with smiles. Exercising his arms animatedly while leading the choir, he became warmer and warmer. The feminine handkerchiefs were woefully inadequate. Finally in desperation during a pause he smilingly excused himself for a moment, returning triumphantly bearing a man-sized brow-mopper. And he was such a good sport as to enjoy the situation as much as the rest.

This choral director interspersed the musical numbers with brief explanations, where appropriate, excusing himself for these asides. Then before the final number he drolly remarked, "I think I feel another speech coming on!" Everyone laughed. He then proceeded to explain the meaning of "Shoogy Shoe," in case some didn't know. Same as "seesaw," he told them, and the rendering of this swinging song was very delightful.

All in all, the musical program was the type which everyone enjoys. One woman said it was far more enjoyable to her than a two-dollar symphony concert heard that same week, for the church choir concert, she explained, contained music she could "understand."

CHAPTER XVI

## SPECIAL CHORAL EVENTS HELP QUICKEN THE SPIRITUAL LIFE

Sometimes choir leaders and "just average singers" are able, through prayer, to break new ground to the glory of God by planning occasionally to enlarge the scope of sacred music activities. Yes, it takes extra time—and special faith—for the undertaking, but when it helps to quicken the spiritual life of a community the result seems worth the effort.

Portland, Ore., was recently blest and stimulated along sacred lines when a Portland Institute of Sacred Music was held there for almost a week in one of the large churches of that city. The course was under the direction of Dr. John Finley Williamson, President of Westminster Choir College, Princeton, N.J., and Director of the noted Westminster Choir.

As a climax to the Institute of Sacred Music,

a choral concert was given on the final Sunday afternoon under the direction of Dr. Williamson. The concert, "A Service of Song and Worship," was relatively unheralded, but vitally significant to church musicians of the city and to others with an appreciation for sacred music, for there were a thousand listeners.

The singing was done by two choirs: One of which had been allowed five hours of rehearsal for the concert; the other—twice that time. In all, there were approximately two hundred voices, and they came from a number of channels functioning through the church: choir directors, church soloists, ministers, and related positions. There were also public music directors and a number of singers who had never appeared in a vocal ensemble before.

THE OREGONIAN, a morning newspaper of Portland, gave excellent space to a report of the event. An excerpt follows:

(Referring to the above, and the limited rehearsal of the participants in the concert) : This is hardly the material upon which the ordinary choir director would venture his reputation for a few hours rehearsing. But Dr. Williamson is evidently no ordinary director; he has more reputation than most; and he has, furthermore, both an idea and a technic. His idea is that the general status of the church would be better if the music were improved; if the right voices functioned where they belong in the right kind of music. Music, he feels, is a worshipful adjunct to the service, which should enlist the participation of everyone from small groups to the entire congregation.

His technic, as one heard Sunday afternoon, is of the comprehensive sort which, in a few hours, brings an unassociated group into perspective as a unified ensemble. He assigned his five-hour group to an assortment of sacred music from a 16th century hymn by Sweelnick to a motet by Sebastian Bach, from "Praise We Sing to Thee," by Haydn, to "Glory Be to Thee," by Rachmaninoff. They sang without accompaniment, they sang true to pitch, their balance was acceptable, and their ensemble was uncommonly good. This, for the time they had worked together and the fact that they are not professional singers, constitutes some kind of a minor miracle.

The ten-hour group, called the Festival Choir, sang "The Passion Trilogy," by Alexander Koshetz. Here were not only balance and a clean ringing adherence to pitch, but tone coloring of some subtlety and noticeable competence in dynamic control.

To be able to say this about a choir so constituted is more than a testimonial to the educative skill of Dr. Williamson, it is also a forecast of improvement in the church and secular ensembles whose members and directors have been a part of the process which saw such admirable fruition Sunday afternoon at the public auditorium.

## Chapter XVII

# THE STORY BACK OF GOSPEL SONGS

### By Flora E. Breck

*(This article originally appeared in the magazine,* The Choir Leader, *published by Lorenz.)*

Dr. W. S. Martin, composer of the music of "God Will Take Care of You," recently gave a two-hour talk in a Portland, Oregon, church concerning gospel song writers and composers, relating also the story back of many of our church songs. He has known intimately most of the great religious song-writers during the past fifty years, especially the older ones, and has studied critically gospel hymns new and old. Dr. Martin, white-haired, benign, has lived approximately three score and ten years, but is so keen and entertaining as to appear much younger, and his audience listened in rapt attention.

He still conducts evangelistic services, running

heavy schedules involving trans-continental trips. His wife, author of the words of "God Will Take Care of You," is now too frail to accompany him, but she is still greatly interested in church music. Their home is in Atlanta, Georgia.

Dr. Martin loves music with all his soul. He had not sung for years in public, but he was prevailed upon to sing one number at the Portland service. His voice was clear and rich. And he admits that he enjoys singing, and declares, "To sing strengthens our faith and warms our hearts."

Dr. Martin inherited his love for beautiful music. His mother was a very notable singer; she once sang with Jenny Lind. "When I Survey the Wondrous Cross" was one of her favorites.

Dr. Martin reminisced concerning J. H. Tenney who composed the music, "We'll Never Say Goodbye in Heaven." He said Tenney was a New England farmer who heartily enjoyed driving his old horse. Although offered a lucrative salary if he would accept a position as director of music in the east he refused to leave his old home.

Dr. Martin when a boy used to wonder how Tenney could compose music. To encourage the boy, Tenney once said to him, "Why don't *you* write a song?" Martin immediately asked a neighbor to write a poem for him. He took a manuscript home, wrestled with it most of the night. By daybreak he had composed a melody for it; and a prouder boy would have been hard to find, for the hymn was published and used in a Sunday-school song book. Dr. Tenney is dead now, but his spirit still lives, for it was he who inspired Dr. Martin to compose music.

Dr. Martin knew personally Elisha Hoffman, who wrote the words of "Glory to His Name," "Leaning on the Everlasting Arms," and a host of other songs. Once Dr. Martin asked Hoffman for some of his compositions and the latter *gave* Martin fifty songs! It is said Hoffman always gave his songs away.

William H. Doane was perhaps the most popular church song writer of his time. He was composer of "Jesus, Keep Me Near the Cross." Dr. Martin knew Doane as a business man in Cincinnati. The latter was very rich, having made a lot of money as a manufacturer of machinery. He wrote the music to "Safe in the Arms of Jesus," and Fanny J. Crosby, the blind poet, wrote the words. One day Dr. Martin said to Fanny Crosby, "How came you to write that hymn?" and she told him the story of how it came to be written.

Mr. Doane came to her office one day and said, "Fanny, I've got a new tune, and I want words for it. I'm in a hurry, and have only three-quarters of an hour to wait!" He proceeded to play the melody, and it so impressed her that the words, as she said, "fairly bubbled out." She had it finished within twenty minutes. Fanny Crosby wrote almost countless song-poems. She was past ninety when she died.

Dr. Martin continued: "I knew Robert Lowry, who wrote, 'Shall We Gather at the River?' He was a Baptist preacher in Brooklyn, New York; he was big, red-headed, homely, but every inch a Christian. A better song writer never lived. Mrs. Annie S. Hawks and Robert Lowry wrote a number of hymns together."

Dr. Martin once visited Mrs. Hawks. She was a small woman, past eighty-five. He met and lunched with her; they talked "shop" and exchanged songs. Lowry, Martin explained, asked her for a poem for the melody, "I Need Thee Every Hour"; and she composed that well-known song-poem.

Dr. Martin said that his wife was married to

him for many years before she realized she had a talent for writing poetry. The first song-poem she wrote was "His Eye Is on the Sparrow." Altogether, Mrs. Martin has written nearly two thousand songs.

One day Dr. and Mrs. Martin were calling on a friend who was bedridden, a chronic invalid. "Don't you feel lonely all by yourself sometimes?" the Martins asked her.

"Not at all," she replied beaming. "When I'm alone I sing because I'm happy, and I sing because I'm free. The eye of God, who sees each sparrow, is on me too," she testified. Mrs. Martin's face lit up. She left the room for a few moments, returning with a paper in her hand. They read the lines to the invalid, a Mrs. Doolittle. The words were "His Eye Is on the Sparrow," a song which is sung around the world today. This hymn was once sung in a Torrey evangelistic meeting attended by fifteen thousand people. The audience insisted that the soloist sing it eight times before they would let him leave the platform. This song has been sung in jails, hospitals, etc., and has brought untold comfort.

William F. Sherwin, who wrote "Break Thou the Bread of Life," was an intimate friend of

Doctor Martin's mother. One time when he was visiting the Martin home he had occasion to see one of Doctor Martin's earlier songs, and he said, "Why don't you come to school to me and study harmony?" Sherwin offered to give his time gratis two evenings a week if Doctor Martin would study. It was arranged, and this young musician studied harmony two evenings a week while he was attending Harvard College.

Doctor Martin knew Mr. E. O. Excell well. He had heard early in his own evangelistic preaching career that Excell was a great Sunday-school song leader. Dr. Martin was conducting an evangelistic campaign in a city one time and invited Excell to be his song leader. After the close of the evening Martin confessed, "Do you know, Mr. Excell, you're the first song leader I've ever engaged to sing for a series of meetings!" Excell smiled. "And do you know," he responded, "you're the first evangelist I ever assisted with the singing!" They both enjoyed the situation hugely. For a long time after that they continued to form this kind of a team, and were most congenial.

Before Martin became converted he went to a Moody and Sankey meeting. D. L. Moody preached his "Good Shepherd" sermon, and Ira

D. Sankey followed it with "The Ninety and Nine." It was sung with deepest feeling, and it was the hearing of this song which led to Martin's conversion. Later on, Martin became well acquainted with Sankey. The latter explained to him how "The Ninety and Nine" came to be written. He felt the melody came from God, for he sang this musical number a month before he transcribed the music on paper. The words were handed to him as a newspaper clipping while he sat on the platform at church. The lines fitted into the theme of the "Good Shepherd" sermon that Moody was preaching that night, and Sankey was asked to sing the words of the poem. He began, not knowing just how it was coming out, nor whether he could remember his melody for the other verses as he came to them. But he seemed to be inspired from above, and gave to the audience this triumphant shepherd hymn— "Rejoice for the Lord brings back His own!" This new song was indeed *born,* not composed, and twenty thousand people were moved to tears as they listened.

Dr. Martin told an amusing incident concerning D. B. Towner in Boston. Martin was then about eighteen, and he carried a poem of his up to Towner to get his estimate of it. "Throw it in the waste basket," Towner advised after perusing it. Years after this, Doctor Martin reminded Towner of the incident. Towner explained, "Oh, I had the big-head then. Since that time I've been living in *God's* grace." And Towner continued to dwell on the "marvelous grace" of God. He it was who composed the hymn music of "Grace Greater than Our Sins."

Martin explained that he had planned to have a visit with Charles H. Gabriel, the world famous song writer. Martin had invited him to meet him in California in September, 1932, but just a few days before going south from Portland, Mr. Gabriel's son sent him word of his father's death.

One of Mr. Gabriel's most noted hymns was "The Glory Song." Dr. Martin stated that Gabriel wrote the music for two hundred of Mrs. Martin's song-poems, and that all of these songs were widely and successfully used by Charles Alexander.

The hour was late, but Dr. Martin was requested to tell how his own "God Will Take Care of You" came to be written. So he explained. In 1904 he was leaving Philadelphia for Winnipeg, Canada. On the way with his wife, Mrs. Martin became sick, and they had to stop off at

Binghamton, New York. He was invited to preach there Sunday night; however, his wife was so ill that he about decided not to accept the invitation. Then their nine-year-old boy spoke up. "Don't you think God can take care of Mother as well with you gone to church as if you were here in the house?" he asked. It was a challenge. Martin preached that night. When he returned home after the sermon his small boy met him at the door with a piece of paper on which his wife had pencilled the words of the hymn she had just written, "God Will Take Care of You."

"Let's dedicate this song to God," one of them said. And so they knelt down by the bedside of his wife. The little boy, too, in his own words prayed, "Lord, you use this song and make it help somebody." The child's prayer has been answered abundantly, for Dr. Martin stated that he has in his possession more than a thousand letters written by people in many lands saying how much they have been blessed by the hymn, "God Will Take Care of You."

Dr. Martin's talk was given in Calvary Tabernacle in Portland, of which Rev. Willard H. Pope is pastor; and the address was livened up throughout by the rendition of verses and choruses and solos of the songs referred to. This church features the "old-time" religious songs over the air in their "Morning Devotional Hour" broadcasts, and the interest of their hearers was deepened by the stories back of these songs.

# Chapter XVIII

## THE WORLD'S HOME SONG

### By Flora E. Breck

(*This article originally appeared in the magazine,* The Choir Herald, *published by Lorenz.*)

When we celebrate Mother's Day, one of the songs which means much to us is the old favorite "Home, Sweet Home," the text of which was written by John Howard Payne. The author of this song lost his mother when he was in his early teens, and after that he never knew again what it means to have a home of his own. It is remarkable that he should have been the man to write what is universally acknowledged as the world's home song.

John Howard was born June 8th, 1791, in New York City, the sixth of nine children born to his parents. While he was still young, the family moved to Easthampton, Long Island, into a house still standing and open to visitors, for it has been bought by the town authorities to perpetuate the memory of John Howard Payne. This house had such an atmosphere and breathed such a spirit of home that it made a deep impression on the boy, which later was to find expression in his world-famous "Home, Sweet Home."

John Howard Payne had a very checkered career. When he was only thirteen years of age, his father placed him as a clerk in a counting house. His talents and impressive personality soon found him friends, who raised funds to help him complete his education, and so he entered Union College in Schenectady. Before he was seventeen he made his first appearance on the stage as an actor and his youth and handsome appearance and the spontaneity of his acting made for immediate success. In 1813 he went to England and remained there for about 20 years. There he wrote, among other things, the text for the play "Clari," which contained the song that was to make him famous. Its first production was in May, 1823, and it has been sung on both sides of the ocean ever since.

In 1832 Payne returned to America and in 1842 was appointed U. S. Consul in Tunis. He died while in office, April 9, 1852. He was never married, and the dream of the home sweet home that seems to have haunted him through the years must have had its origin in the home of his childhood days. The second verse of his song carries with it special tenderness and pathos.

I gaze on the moon as I tread the drear wild,
And feel that my mother now thinks of her child,
As she looks on that moon from our own cottage door,
Thro the woodbine, whose fragrance shall cheer me no
    more.

## Chapter XIX

## UNIQUE "HYMN-SING," HONORING FANNY CROSBY AND THE BLIND

A Sunday evening song service centering around the hymns of Fanny J. Crosby, the blind hymn-writer, was held at the Rose City Park Methodist Church at Portland, Oregon, recently. The blind people of Portland were honor guests, and the service drew a good crowd.

The Fanny J. Crosby Memorial Song Book was used by the congregation, and the choir sang effectively: "Though Your Sins Be As Scarlet," "To the Work," "My Saviour First of All," all hymns written by her.

A talk regarding Fanny Crosby's contribution to hymnology was given by the pastor, Reverend Fred C. Taylor. He mentioned that she was born in 1820 and died in 1915, that she was blind since six weeks of age, and wrote 7,000 songs, poems and hymns. She wrote under some two hundred pen names, using these because so many of her hymns frequently appeared in a single song book.

The "Epworth Choir" added much to the worshipful atmosphere of the service. Gowned in black, with white surplice, they occupied the front of the church just underneath an illuminated cross of white light, touched at the back with blood-red light.

Miss Marguerite Carney, a blind young woman, having a marvelously clear soprano, sang, "Come Ye Blessed," by Scott. There was a vocal solo by a blind man; and Malcolm Medlar, blind organist, played several selections.

B. F. Irvine, blind editor of the OREGON JOURNAL, gave a powerful talk, emphasizing the value of the church to the community. This "white-maned" man (he goes bareheaded almost all the time), one of the well-known civic leaders in Portland and the Northwest, has a deep appreciation for music. He paid high tribute to Miss Carney's voice, "the loveliest in the United States," he declared.

A young man from the Oregon Blind Trade School gave a talk on the accomplishments of the blind through training, and showed baskets and other samples of their work. He explained how these people are able to make salable brushes, brooms, mops; and do chair-caning, etc., after "learning the art of being blind." He urged patronage from the public where these items were needed, in order to help the blind to become self-supporting. "Blind piano-tuners are among the most skillful in this line of work," he declared.

The pastor spoke lovingly and appreciatively of these "artists" who had come to participate in the song service of the evening. His subject was "The Divine Friend of the Blind."

A page of Braille printing was given to each member of the congregation present, being torn from an old copy of READER'S DIGEST, which magazine is regularly issued in Braille for the benefit of the blind. Church-workers furnished free transportation to the blind visitors at the church, having no other means of attending the meeting. This Fanny Crosby Memorial service gave much joy and proved a great blessing, for both sightless and those who see, like to hear the old-time Gospel hymns.

## Chapter XX

# HYMNS WE LOVE

In this book I have mentioned some of the hymn-titles which song *leaders* have chosen for worship services. Now, may I refer briefly to the kind of hymns I personally like—the kind I find helpful and satisfying. I mean the hymns which sing themselves over and over *within,* long after choir or congregation have sung the last note. When snatches of hymns echo again and again through Tuesday and Wednesday while we are engaged in mundane duties—then we are likely to know that the Sunday worship service was rightly planned. Hymn music is not merely an *adjunct* to living. Some of us feel it is *life* itself!

The kind of songs which have this quality are hymns of dignity, beauty, joy. I mention *dignity* first because it seems so important. The light jingle-type of songs sung frequently at religious gatherings do not seem the most worthy kind either for adult or youthful congregations. Yes, I realize that many children and some young people sing that type almost to the exclusion of the stately, serious kind; but song leaders of insight realize that *tastes can be cultivated.* Sometimes it is well to let teen-agers sing their favorite songs—even though the selections do not quite measure up to the ideals of their leaders. If, *in addition,* the young are "exposed" to the better type of church hymns, many of the lusty singers will eventually *ask* for the more worthy type of songs. (I believe I have referred before to the very small child who loved and sang—most often of all—"Oh Come All Ye Faithful." In her case the mother saw to it that the five-year-old frequently heard the stately type of hymns.)

Where children are slow to take up with the beautiful kind of hymns it is sometimes the fault of their song leader at church school. Perhaps he does not pick out the best songs nor suggest they sing them in a worshipful manner. Many of us have heard Sunday school children fairly *yell,* to the accompaniment of thumping feet, while they were "whooping it up." That, of course, is not worship. If the song leader draws the attention of the children to the beauty of certain lines of a hymn, or the musical setting, or the circumstances under which the hymn came to be written,—all that helps instill respect and love for the song being sung. The taste for better music on the part of *adults,* also, can be improved similarly.

To me, the ideal type of sacred song is the kind addressed to God. In other words, the prayer-type of hymn. Some of us, indeed, wish that a larger proportion of hymns were of this kind. Somehow we feel that in singing or listening to these we are drawn closer to God—and He to us.

And, speaking of the appropriate type of sacred songs, let us emphasize especially the kind where the musical setting is in keeping with the words. Occasionally an otherwise beautiful hymn-poem has been wedded to a light melody—so light that it seems off-key for a real worship service. However, fortunately, most hymn-lyrics are set to music which seems to "belong."

One way we may be assured as to whether a sacred song is the most desirable type is to know whether it has proved *durable* through the years. Many of the truly beautiful hymns have lived through the ages—and are still sung with joy. And, since there are so many of this type, let us include a goodly number of these in planning worship services. For instance, hymns like "Fairest Lord Jesus" and "When I Survey the Wondrous Cross." These are not only *sweet* hymns,—

they are *significant* ones. Song leaders have a heavy responsibility. Both choir and congregation will enjoy increasingly this type of hymn if such songs are chosen frequently.

## Chapter XXI

# CHARLES H. GABRIEL'S SAYINGS ABOUT CHURCH MUSIC AND CHOIRS

The late Charles H. Gabriel was one of the most prolific of hymn composers. He was always advocating higher standards of workmanship for musicians; he was considered an authority in this line, and his services as a speaker on Gospel music, song-leading, and congregational singing were often in demand in various parts of the country. Finally, the Rodeheaver Company compiled in pamphlet form the text of some of his lectures, and it is to that Company I am indebted for permission to quote from portions of these. I quote as follows:

## *THE CHURCH CHOIR*

### By Charles H. Gabriel

Music makes us think of God. If a song is not a prayer it has no place in the song book or hymnal. All the finest emotions of the human breast must find expression in rhythm and music, and every worthy sentiment naturally has a religious aspect and counterpart.

Reverence is the foundation of worship. It is written in the heart of every true Christian and will show itself in his manner; therefore, the first requisite of a good choir singer is reverence. The manner of a singer is more in evidence than the music he helps to make. There must be a spirit of service, whether the singer is or is not paid. *A salaried choir singer is no more objectionable than a salaried minister, so long as the motive is sincere.* A good choir singer is one who sings to render a willing service to the church of his choice.

The choir singer who does not love music for what it stands for has no place in singing for the good he may do. One who cannot sacrifice gladly the time and inconvenience demanded by the regular rehearsal, or cannot enter into the part he is expected to fill, loses a blessing that thousands would pay any possible price to realize. The good choir singer will sing forth his praise to God as though none but himself were worshiping, and not as a *diva* warbles the trills and roulades of a Bellini or a Meyerbeer.

A timid singer is never successful. At the other extreme we find one whose ego protrudes to a degree distressing to all. This type arises, song book in hand, and defies the congregation to render him aught but praise. Such a singer immediately severs all art relations with his audience, robs himself of any eulogium which might become his, arouses an antagonistic, unreverent attitude on the part of the auditory and loses sight of the object for which he sings.

A good choir singer is one who is in sympathy with the congregation; one who improves in musical knowledge and skill and who keeps in vital relation to the art of music; one who is prompt at rehearsal and never absent except for unavoidable cause; one who sees and does his duty as a singer.

There are various kinds of choirs—paid choirs, volunteer choirs, junior, senior, chorus, quartet, male and female choirs, but *the ideal aggregation is a choir of young people whose names are on the roster of the church in which they sing.*

Mistakes are made by all, from the organist to those in the pews. The organist makes a mistake in leading instead of following the singers; in failing to watch and be governed by the chorister; in "covering" the soloist by loud playing; in making offertory selections which are not in sympathy with the subject of the occasion; in introducing chords or cadences which are not found on the printed page of the music being sung; in extemporizing flighty interludes between the stanzas of a devotional hymn, and in playing a jazz or "ragtime" postlude at the close of the Sunday evening service.

The choir singer makes a mistake by being absent from rehearsal; by being late on practice occasions; by finding fault with the selections of the chorister; by inattention to his instructions; by whispering, giggling, chewing gum, reading or sleeping during the sermon.

The chorister makes a mistake when he appears before his singers without a perfectly arranged program for the occasion for which they are to rehearse; when he loses the dignity which should characterize his position; when he is cross or lacking in adroitness and skill; when he gesticulates wildly, stamps his feet, shouts at his singers or makes a clown of himself.

The pastor makes a mistake when he fails to meet with the choir occasionally to speak a word of encouragement; when he does not make known to the chorister, before rehearsal time, his sermon-subjects and the hymns he desires sung; when he does not take vital interest in both the music and the singers of his choir.

The church member makes a mistake by criticizing song or singer; by coming in late and taking a seat during the singing of a solo; by reading during the anthem—thus showing discourtesy to the conscientious work of the entire choir; by failing to join in the singing of every congregational hymn; by withholding moral and financial support of the choir, the members of which, as a rule, give their services faithfully and gratuitously, although often at great disadvantage and sacrifice.

A good choir is a progressive choir. It is not satisfied with merely "something to sing" at the preaching service. Its ambition is to climb to a higher plane of artistic development and excellence. It does not spurn the easy grade of music that is well within its ability to render in a musicianly manner, nor does it attempt to sing publicly a difficult classic until its intricacies are thoroughly mastered.

What study is to the sermon, rehearsal is to the song. The rehearsal may well be more than its name implies; it may be a class in the art of music if the chorister so wills it, and has tact and ability. The choir may elevate its own choice in music and overcome its deficiencies in theory and practice, and be ever growing in its art.

A good choir will have reverence for God, cooperation with the pastor, sympathy with the congregation, and growth in usefulness and service. . . .

The choir is a unit, composed of several, and should act, think, and sing as one person. The minister leads in prayer and sermon, the choir in song. One is seriously handicapped without the other. The stranger in town does not usually ask, "Where will I hear the ablest sermon?" His question is more often, "Where will I hear the best music?"

Music and sermon are, in a sense, synonymous and occupy a common plane of importance in public worship. If the preacher is spiritual and aggressive the choir will catch his vision and rise to his excellence. As the church authorities support and sustain the preacher, in like manner they should encourage and uphold the choir morally and financially.

There is not a church in the land that cannot be filled if the pastor and choir will join hands and "go out into the highways and byways and compel them to come in that my house may be filled."

## THE CHURCH CHOIR LEADER

### By Charles H. Gabriel

. . . To be a successful leader requires adroitness, skill, swift and practical judgment. Singers do not always appreciate the complexities that lie in his pathway nor sympathize with the maneuvers he must employ to preserve the peace and harmony which is absolutely essential to his success. While he is engaged with some difficulty encountered by any one of the parts which need separate drill, the other singers relax into a discussion of personalities and local happenings, so that by the time he is ready to resume general training the "atmosphere" has changed, and concentration of thought broken. Valuable time spent in reconcentration is lost, not to mention the test to which his native temperament has been subjected or his patience tried.

. . . It is a deplorable fact that the direction of church music matters is usually left with committees incompetent to judge what is best. There are exceptions to this rule, of course, but generally speaking, it is true. Music should be under the direction of those who have a higher conception of musical art and thought than the average church member. Possibly the time is coming when we shall have a minister or master of music in the church, one who is qualified by education and by lofty ideals to attend to the needs of the congregation.

The anthem is for the few, the hymn for all. Next to his Bible the choir leader should be acquainted with the hymn book. He should know by name the tunes of the different metres and be able to sing them in their correct pitch without the aid of an instrument.

Every choir leader should devote at least twenty to thirty minutes at each rehearsal to the practice of the music of the old masters. There is no better music in print. Much has been written by more modern authors whose names are familiar to professional singers, but it is, comparatively, poorly written and lacks the melody, harmony, and spontaneity so prominent and delightful in the works of Handel, Haydn, and others.

After a few evenings' drill on these old classics each individual singer will be surprised to realize how much easier it is to satisfy the most exacting demands of the leader for the rendition of the average anthem. The successful leader will never attempt to sing, publicly, music that is impracticable. The "Hallelujah Chorus" cannot be satisfactorily sung by a choir of the average number of singers. By reason of the same argument many other great selections must not be attempted, but —the benefit resulting from the practice and drill on these old masterpieces cannot be overestimated.

No choir leader should despise the easy anthem because it is easy. Too often his selection is so difficult that it monopolizes the mind and ability of each member of the choir to the extent that its performance is entirely robbed of the element of worship. This condition is manifest by the congregation and has a depressing influence upon the minister, not to speak of the deductions made by the stranger who happens to be in the audience. The choir leader should not be prejudiced regarding the different authors of music. What he likes, the congregation may not be pleased with; his favorite may be distasteful to his singers. He should be broadminded enough to sing the best, notwithstanding who wrote it. Many leaders sing over and over such pieces as have become so well known to congregations through repetition that all interest in them has been lost. Why sing only well-known and threadbare selections simply because other choirs sing them? Why not rather take the initiative and popularize something new?

Give the new writer a chance—you will need him and his music some day—and that very soon. Give him a hearing now and encourage him to prepare the music you will be obliged to sing to-morrow, for it is the young composer to whom you must look for the supply of the future. Wagner surprised the world after it became convinced of his genius. All the young writer asks is an impartial hearing; and, unless he is noticed and his music heard, in ten years from now the choir must sing the same music it sings to-day.

A large majority of choirs are volunteer organizations. Many of the singers are not music readers. Few have had former experience in singing. For this reason the music committee should withhold nothing that will aid, encourage, and sustain the singers. If a competent leader cannot be found in the church, an experienced one should be employed. The conscientious leader will begin training such choirs with an easy but effective grade of music, and as advancement is made by the singers his judgment will dictate an aggressive policy.

We are all more or less interested in that in which we have a part. A twenty or thirty minute song service preceding the evening sermon will attract people who will listen respectfully to a sermon they would not otherwise go to hear. Not a service of concert selections, but one of plain, simple, gospel music and hymns; songs that carry a message; songs that lift one out of the gloom of everyday life into the bright sunlight of hope; songs that inspire one to nobler things; that stimulate faith, and reveal a new vision of the better world we all hope to gain. Such evenings will furnish the choir with additional opportunity for advanced work. Care should be exercised, however, that the congregation is not deprived of a large share in the program, which should not consist of old and familiar songs alone. Congregations, like individuals, enjoy a new song occasionally. . . .

When the time comes in which the choir leader, choir singer, pew and pulpit lay aside all petty criticism and strive together as with one mind and one heart to make more attractive the musical service of the Master, then —and not until then—will all bickerings cease, praise be made comely and pleasant and the Lord's house be filled.

## THE EVANGELISTIC SONG LEADER

### By Charles H. Gabriel

First and always the evangelistic song director must be a consecrated Christian. He need not be a soloist; his mission is to get others to sing. He is responsible to the people to the degree of his leadership.

It is laudable for song leaders to employ that agency which will arouse the interest of the people that attention may be more definitely drawn to the sermon that is to follow, but unless their efforts are based on experience and good judgment they distort melodic interpretation of gospel truth.

No leader will become successful through mere imitation of another. He must have originality and initiative. He may profit by the example and experience of others, but will never attain eminence alone through the use of methods originated and characterized by someone else. He must be at least reasonably educated in literature and the theory and practice of rudimentary music. It would be a great help to him if he knew harmony. He should be a good drill master and an expert in handling singers and congregations. He should be well acquainted with his song book and the denominational hymnals, and be able to select the right song for any occasion that may suddenly arise, and to choose it wisely and promptly. He should not try to lead with his voice. Neither should he imitate a windmill with his arms, nor a contortionist with his body. He need not beat time by absolutely correct theoretical motions, as does the conductor of a symphony orchestra, but his motions should be strict, decisive, and have a meaning so obvious that the uninitiated may understand his every wish.

"He talked too much" has been the cause of many an evangelistic song leader's downfall. The desire to be "funny"; to illustrate a condition with a strange story; to tell an anecdote connected with a song, the truth of which he cannot establish; . . . and a score of other themes which distract attention from the one important subject—praise, is very unwise.

To assure every choir he leads that it is the best he has ever presided over is untruthful.

To comment after each stanza of a song, use the personal pronoun overfrequently, or to ask the people to "sing for me this time" is egotistical.

To criticize the singing of a prayer song, or browbeat the people into singing at a furious *tempo* the old hymns they have been accustomed to sing in a religious manner is sacrilege.

118

The old adage, "Familiarity breeds contempt," is superlatively true when applied to the mannerisms of the song leader. He should have the native ability to get the best results from the singers under his command without resort to harshness and foolish criticism.

Very few evangelistic song conductors are, in the true sense, musicians. Fewer still are producers—composers—of music. Seldom is one a real drillmaster or a proficient soloist; many of them are unable to read music at sight, fluently. Many of them have been "discovered" and drawn into the work without proper training or sufficient observation, and, therefore possess only natural cleverness as leaders. They lack the convincing personality that proclaims absolute authority. That there are exceptional cases is apparent, but he fails in his duty who does not constantly exalt the standard of sacred music, or who uses it to exploit his personal ability as a leader. He is not worthy of holding the position he occupies who "plays to the gallery" through the agency of gospel song.

A few names have been indelibly written into the history of gospel song leadership. Ira D. Sankey and E. O. Excell achieved prominence and fame without the aid of the present-day evangelistic choir with all its advantages. The audience was their choir and their singing was congregational. Charles M. Alexander was, perhaps, the first to organize and popularize the revival choir, and to Homer A. Rodeheaver belongs the distinction of having directed the largest sacred song choruses of all time.

Too often the song leader is disposed to abuse the use of these splendid organizations in that he loses sight of the real purpose for which they are organized—to lead the people in song. It is so easy, under revival conditions, to get service and effect from a choir, and so difficult to obtain complete response from the audience that the congregation gets too little attention.

It is but repetition to state that upon the shoulders of the evangelistic song director lies the possibilities for advancing and perpetuating sacred music. His field of labor is wide and his opportunities of reaching and training large numbers of people multiplies his responsibility over and over.

## DEDUCTIONS AND CONCLUSIONS

### By Charles H. Gabriel

. . . Art should be recognized in the church service, and the nearer it is to perfection the better, but it must be accompanied by faith and love in the soul of the singer for spiritual results. When this is not true the congregation is disappointed, the singer fails, men are not blest, and God is not praised. The harmony between art and religion must be held inviolable.

The prayer meeting could be made vastly more interesting and attractive to young people if it were more characterized by music. The day of long-faced religion has gone by. The happiest person living to-day is the consecrated Christian. . . .

(AUTHOR'S NOTE: "O That Will be Glory," otherwise known as "The Glory Song," is perhaps Mr. Gabriel's best-known hymn. Others of his well-known hymns—music composed by him—are as follows, all being included in Rodeheaver's "Victorious Service Songs" hymn-book: Brighten the Corner Where You Are, His Eye Is on the Sparrow, I Need Jesus, The Way of the Cross Leads Home, Higher Ground, Since Jesus Came into My Heart, Help Somebody Today, Where the Gates Swing Outward Never, etc.)

## Chapter XXII

# THE PLACE OF PRAYER IN
# THE SINGER'S WORK

The ministry of music in church work is so
important that those who sing should pray constantly for God's special blessing upon the selections which are used. An earnest church soloist
whom I knew years ago told me that she did not
*dare* to undertake her part in the service without
special prayer. In talking before a group of chor-
isters, a great conductor once said: "Be sure to
pray before you lead"; and the same leader often
used to remind his choir members: "Pray before
you sing—*it pays.*"

As a help to the choir leader in choosing appropriate selections, it is always wise to confer with
the minister as to the theme of the sermon planned
for the next Sunday; but sometimes a leader will
feel impelled to make a last minute change in the
selections planned for use by the choir or by the
congregation. On one occasion, a certain choir
leader had requested the soloist to sing a particu-

lar selection at the close of the service; but as he listened to the sermon, he felt impelled to change the plans which had been made, and instead of the solo to have the choir sing, "O Master, Let Me Walk with Thee." At first the idea seemed to him a fleeting impulse; but later, as he felt that the change in plan was divinely guided, he asked the choir to sing that well-loved hymn as the closing selection. (As the soloist was a deeply spiritual person, he had no misgiving as to her willingness to concur in the change of plan.) He learned later that at least two people in the congregation that day were definitely influenced by the singing of that hymn.

The late Charles H. Gabriel (previously referred to), who composed hymns for more than fifty years, once declared: "The church singer must not expect to please everyone. While singing the Gospel there should be in the mind of the singer *no thought of pleasing anyone!* [1] The consecrated church singer is as truly 'set apart' to sing the Gospel as the ordained preacher is to preach it. Both have the same message to deliver, and the one is the right hand of power to the other. The song prepares the way for the sermon, and the sermon opens the door for the song. The

[1] Except the Master, of course.—F.E.B.

singer and the minister must be in perfect harmony. A singer should analyze and study his song as the preacher meditates on his sermon. He should have a generous *repertoire* from which to select just the subject the occasion demands. All people are more or less sensitive to music. Music seems to be the connecting link between heaven and earth. It makes us think of God, and the moments of song should be as sacred as the time of prayer. As the sermon is pure and uplifting in its effect, so must the song be spiritual and worshipful if its mission is fulfilled."

Membership in a well-conducted choir constitutes an opportunity for a deeply spiritual experience for those who belong to the group. The words of many of the hymns and anthems which are used in rehearsals deal with Christian experience in a very personal way, and repeated rehearsals of themes of special beauty may be a very moving experience for the participants. The choir leader should frequently remind his members of the importance of undergirding their music with prayer; and to this end the rehearsals should begin and close with prayer.

CHAPTER XXIII

# REFERENCES ON *CHOIRS*
# AND *CHOIR LEADERS*

This book does not contain a bibliography. Instead, I would suggest you visit the music room of your Public Library where you will almost certainly find a wealth of helpful and stimulating material, whether you are choir member or choir leader—or just someone who appreciates sacred songs. Possibly your music librarian will be able to direct you to a rack of the new books on music recently purchased. Some patrons like to find the "very latest." Or, if you have difficulty finding the special phases of music you are interested in, ask a library assistant. She will gladly help you. If the wanted books or pamphlets, etc., are not found on the library shelves, possibly they are in "the stacks." Library aides are exceedingly glad to be of service in procuring the needed publications. Books heavy, books light—books old and new—are yours for the asking.

In our Portland Public Library—and in many

such institutions—there is quite a section devoted to works on hymnology: biographies of hymn composers and hymn-writers, etc. You will also probably find books which tell how certain hymns came to be written, words and music. Just to mention one of the newer titles, "Forty Gospel Hymn Stories," written by George W. Sanville, manager of The Rodeheaver Hall-Mack Company, of Winona Lake, Indiana, has enjoyed *great* popularity—and still is going strong. Incidentally, the author, Mr. Sanville, probably knows more about hymnology than any other living person. Because of his wide experience with hymnals and his broad knowledge of hymns, composers, and writers of the old and new songs, he was recently honored by religious leaders throughout the United States.

But, to return to the subject of choir publications, be sure to ask your librarian about the choir and church music magazines. Our Portland Public Library subscribes to the following little periodicals published by Lorenz Publishing Company, Dayton, Ohio: THE CHOIR LEADER, which furnishes an anthem for every Sunday of the year; THE CHOIR HERALD, another monthly magazine; and THE VOLUNTEER CHOIR, which contains the easiest selections of the three periodicals. These magazines are published simultaneously, and contain valuable suggestions for choir directors and choir members. Members of the congregation also find profit in the articles published from time to time. For instance, recently (if I recall correctly) the Lorenz Company mentioned in an article, that people, in singing, should breathe in through the *mouth* instead of just the nose, as the person doesn't take in the air *fast enough* through the nose to do the most effective singing. Many amateur singers will find invaluable pointers by keeping up with their reading. Inexperienced choir directors, too (as well as others), will find worthwhile suggestions in library periodicals for getting along smoothly with members of their organizations. And, of course, many technical matters are also covered for the benefit of church musicians. No matter what subject we are interested in, we should constantly strive to improve our knowledge if we would grow.

I know of a flower hybridizer—high up in his profession—busy early and late—who takes time to chat with the most humble farmer who visits his place. I once asked the flower fancier how he found time to visit at such length with so-and-so. He explained that he hadn't time *not* to, that he gained some knowledge from every single grower who came his way. He continued, "I've *got* to listen, for I want to learn better ways of doing things." And I saw that this characteristic—as well as his genuine kindliness—was one secret of his success,—for "no man liveth to himself." As long as life lasts we must be on the alert to *learn!*

# HYMNS

# Abide With Me

H.F. LYTE

W. H. MONK

1. A - bide with me! fast falls the e - ven - tide;
2. Swift to its close ebbs out life's lit - tle day;
3. I need Thy pres - ence ev - 'ry pass-ing hour,
4. Hold Thou Thy cross be - fore my clos-ing eyes;

The dark-ness deep - ens— Lord, with me a - bide!
Earth's joys grow dim, its glo - ries pass a - way;
What but Thy grace can foil the temp - ter's pow'r?
Shine thro' the gloom, and point me to the skies;

When oth - er help - ers fail, and com forts flee,
Change and de - cay in all a - round I see;
Who, like Thy self, my guide and stay can be?
Heav'n's morn-ing breaks, and earth's vain shad ows flee!

Help of the help - less, O a - bide with me!
O Thou, who chang-est not, a - bide with me!
Thro' cloud and sun-shine, O a - bide with me!
In life, in death, O Lord, a - bide with me!

131

## America.

S. F. Smith.

Henry Carey.

1. My coun-try! 'tis of thee, Sweet land of lib-er-ty,
2. My na-tive coun-try, thee, Land of the no-ble free,

Of thee I sing: Land where my fa-thers died! Land of the
Thy name I love; I love thy rocks and rills, Thy woods and

Pil-grims' pride! From ev-ery mount-ain side Let free-dom ring!
tem-pled hills; My heart with rapt-ure thrills, Like that a-bove.

3 Let music swell the breeze,
And ring from all the trees
  Sweet freedom's song:
Let mortal tongues awake;
Let all that breathe partake;
Let rocks their silence break,—
  The sound prolong.

4 Our fathers' God, to thee,
Author of liberty,
  To thee we sing;
Long may our land be bright
With freedom's holy light;
Protect us by thy might,
  Great God, our King.

# Christ, the Lord, is Risen Today

Worgan

Charles Wesley

From Lyra Davidica

1. Christ the Lord is ris'n to day,— Al - le - lu - ia!
2. Lives a - gain our glo - rious King: Al - le - lu - ia!
3. Love's re-deem-ing work is done, Al - le - lu - ia!
4. Soar we now, where Chrst has led,— Al - le - lu - ia!

Sons of men and an-gels say:— Al - le - lu - ia!
Where, O death, is now thy sting? Al - le - lu - ia!
Fought the fight, the bat-tle won;— Al - le - lu - ia!
Fol-l'wing our ex - alt - ed Head; Al - le - lu - ia!

Raise your joys and tri-umphs high, Al - le - lu - ia!
Dy - ing once, He all doth save: Al - le - lu - ia!
Death in vane for - bids Him rise; Al - le - lu - ia!
Made like Him, like Him we rise; Al - le - lu - ia!

Sing ye_heav'ns, and earth re-ply,_ Al - le - lu - ia!
Where thy vic - to - ry, O grave? Al - le - lu - ia!
Christ has o - pened Par - a - dise._ Al - le - lu - ia!
Ours the cross, the grave, the skies. Al - le - lu - ia!

# Fling Out the Banner

### (Waltham, L.M.)

G.W. DOANE                    J. B. CALKIN

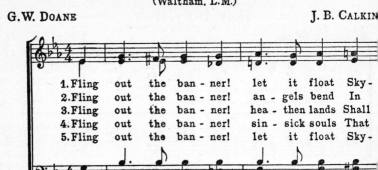

1. Fling out the ban-ner! let it float Sky-
2. Fling out the ban-ner! an-gels bend In
3. Fling out the ban-ner! hea-then lands Shall
4. Fling out the ban-ner! sin-sick souls That
5. Fling out the ban-ner! let it float Sky-

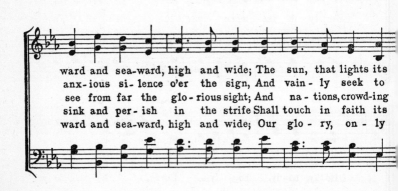

ward and sea-ward, high and wide; The sun, that lights its
anx-ious si-lence o'er the sign, And vain-ly seek to
see from far the glo-rious sight; And na-tions, crowd-ing
sink and per-ish in the strife Shall touch in faith its
ward and sea-ward, high and wide; Our glo-ry, on-ly

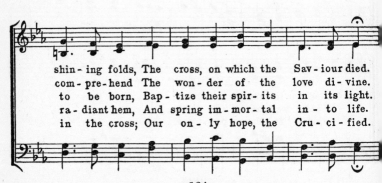

shin-ing folds, The cross, on which the Sav-iour died.
com-pre-hend The won-der of the love di-vine.
to be born, Bap-tize their spir-its in its light.
ra-diant hem, And spring im-mor-tal in-to life.
in the cross; Our on-ly hope, the Cru-ci-fied.

134

# Holy, Holy, Holy

REGINALD HEBER                                                    Rev. J. B. DYKES

1. Ho-ly, ho-ly, ho-ly,— Lord God Al-might-y!
2. Ho-ly, ho-ly, ho-ly! all the saints a-dore Thee,
3. Ho-ly, ho-ly, ho-ly,— Lord God Al-might-y!

Ear-ly in the morn-ing our song shall rise to Thee;
Cast-ing down their gold-en crowns a-round the glass-y sea;
All Thy works shall praise Thy name, in earth, and sky, and sea;

Ho-ly, ho-ly, ho-ly,— mer-ci-ful and might-y!
Cher-u-bim and ser-a-phim fall-ing down be-for Thee,
Ho-ly, ho-ly, ho-ly,— Lord— God Al-might-y!

God in three per-sons,— bless-ed Trin-i-ty!
Which wert, and art, and— ev-er-more shalt be.
God in three per-sons,— bless-ed Trin-i-ty!

135

# It Came Upon The Midnight Clear

Edwin H. Sears

Richard S. Willis

1. It came up-on the mid-night clear, That glo-rious song of old,—
2. Still thro' the clo-ven skies they come, With peace-ful wings un-furled;
3. For lo! the days are has-t'ning on, By proph-ets seen of old,—

From an-gels bend-ing near the earth, To touch their harps of gold:
And still their heav'n-ly mu-sic floats O'er all the wear-y world:
When with the ev - er cir-cling years Shall come the time fore-told,—

"Peace on the earth, good-will to men From heav'n's all-gra-cious King;"
A - bove its sad and low-ly plains They bend on hov-'ring wing,
When the new heav'n and earth shall own The Prince of Peace their King,

The world in sol-emn still-ness lay To hear the an-gels sing.
And ev - er o'er its Ba-bel sounds The bless-ed an-gels sing.
And the whole world send back the song Which now the an-gels sing.

# Jesus is Alive
## Easter Salutation

FLORA E. BRECK

NOEL BENSON

Joyfully

*mf*

Je-sus is a-live this morn-ing, Hope has come to hearts a - new; Ev'ry tomb of night and sad-ness May be-come a gate to glad-ness; Je-sus is a-live this morn-ing;

*mf*

*poco rit.*  *p*

He speaks to you, He speaks to you.
He speaks, he speaks to you.

He speaks to you.

Copyright, 1949, by Lorenz Publishing Co., in "The Volunteer Choir" for March, 1949.
International copyright.
Sg. Sp. No. 2-48.
Used by permission.

# Joy to the World

I. WATTS

G. F. HANDEL

1. Joy to the world! the Lord is come; Let earth receive her King; Let ev'ry heart prepare Him room, And heav'n and nature sing, And heav'n and nature sing, And heav'n, and heav'n and nature sing.

2. Joy to the world! the Savior reigns; Let men their songs employ; While fields and floods, rocks, hills, and plains, Repeat the sounding joy, Repeat the sounding joy, Repeat, repeat the sounding joy.

3. No more let sin and sorrow grow, Nor thorns infest the ground; He comes to make His blessings flow Far as the curse is found, Far as the curse is found, Far as, far as the curse is found.

4. He rules the world with truth and grace, And makes the nations prove The glories of His righteousness, And wonders of His love, And wonders of His love, And wonders, wonders of His love.

# My Faith Looks Up To Thee

RAY PALMER

Dr. LOWELL MASON

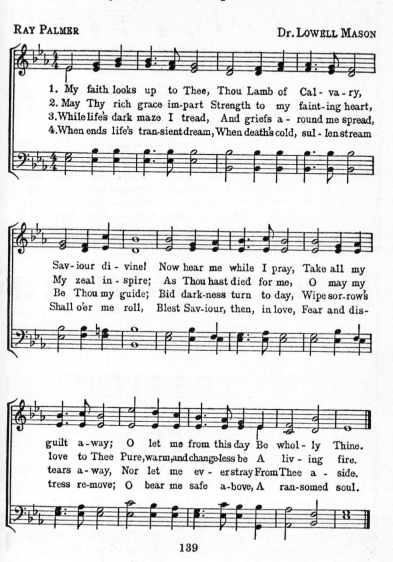

1. My faith looks up to Thee, Thou Lamb of Cal-va-ry,
2. May Thy rich grace im-part Strength to my faint-ing heart,
3. While life's dark maze I tread, And griefs a-round me spread,
4. When ends life's tran-sient dream, When death's cold, sul-len stream

Sav-iour di-vine! Now hear me while I pray, Take all my
My zeal in-spire; As Thou hast died for me, O may my
Be Thou my guide; Bid dark-ness turn to day, Wipe sor-row's
Shall o'er me roll, Blest Sav-iour, then, in love, Fear and dis-

guilt a-way; O let me from this day Be whol-ly Thine.
love to Thee Pure, warm, and change-less be A liv-ing fire.
tears a-way, Nor let me ev-er stray From Thee a-side.
tress re-move; O bear me safe a-bove, A ran-somed soul.

# O Master, Let Me Walk with Thee

WASHINGTON GLADDEN

H. PERCY SMITH

1. O Mas-ter, let me walk with Thee
2. Help me the slow of heart to move
3. Teach me Thy pa-tience! still with Thee
4. In hope that sends a shin-ing ray

In low-ly paths of ser - vice free;
By some clear, win - ning word of love;
In clos - er, dear - er com - pa - ny,
Far down the fu - ture's broad-'ning way,

Tell me Thy se - cret; help me bear The
Teach me the way - ward feet to stay, And
In work that keeps faith sweet and strong, In
In peace that on - ly Thou canst give, With

strain of toil, the fret of care.
guide them in the home - ward way.
trust that tri - umphs o - ver wrong.
Thee, O Mas - ter, let me live.

# Silent Night! Holy Night!

JOSEPH MOHR

FRANZ GRUBER

1. Si - lent night! Ho - ly night! All is dark, save the light Yon - der, where they sweet vig - ils keep, O'er the Babe who in si - lent sleep. Rests in heav - en - ly peace,— Rests— in heav - en - ly peace.—

2. Si - lent night! Peace - ful night! Dark - ness flies, all is light; Shep - herds hear— the an - gels sing, "Al - le - lu - ia! hail— the King! Christ the Sav - ior is born,— Je - sus the Sav - ior is born".—

3. Si - lent night! Ho - ly night! Guid - ing Star, lend thy light! See the East - ern wise— men bring Gifts and hom - age to— our King! Christ the Sav - ior is born,— Je - sus the Sav - ior is born!—

4. Si - lent night! Ho - li - est night! Won - drous Star, lend thy light! With the an - gels let— us sing Al - le - lu - ia to— our King! Christ the Sav - ior is born,— Je - sus the Sav - ior is born!—

# When I Survey the Wondrous Cross

ISAAC WATTS

Arr. by LOWELL MASON

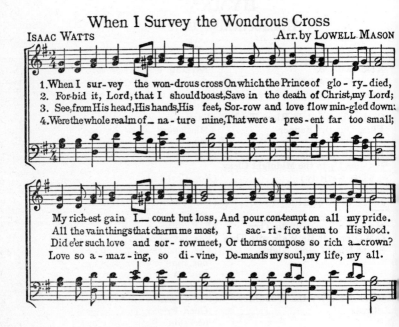

1. When I sur-vey the won-drous cross On which the Prince of glo-ry died,
2. For-bid it, Lord, that I should boast, Save in the death of Christ, my Lord;
3. See, from His head, His hands, His feet, Sor-row and love flow min-gled down:
4. Were the whole realm of na-ture mine, That were a pres-ent far too small;

My rich-est gain I count but loss, And pour con-tempt on all my pride.
All the vain things that charm me most, I sac-ri-fice them to His blood.
Did e'er such love and sor-row meet, Or thorns compose so rich a crown?
Love so a-maz-ing, so di-vine, De-mands my soul, my life, my all.

# HYMNS
## (Alphabetically Indexed)

(NOTE: If interested in hymns, choruses, etc., for children or others, I would suggest you refer to the songs contained also in my books: "Worship Services and Programs for Beginners," "Church School Chats," and "Special Day Programs and Selections.")